The Webmaster's Handbook

Perl Power for your Web Server

JOIN US ON THE INTERNET VIA WWW, GOPHER, FTP OR EMAIL:

WWW:	http://www.thomson.com
GOPHER:	gopher.thomson.com
FTP:	ftp.thomson.com
EMAIL:	findit@kiosk.thomson.com

WebExtra^{sm}

WebExtra gives added value by providing updated and additional information about topics discussed in this book. Items included in the WebExtra for *The Webmaster's Handbook* are:

- All example programs (also included on the CD-ROM), plus updates as necessary
- The Webmaster's Handbook Hotlist, containing all URLs from the book (to be updated as necessary)
- PostScript source for the HTML Reference Guide
- PostScript source for the Perl Reference Guide
- Selections from the book in HTML format
- A separate 'Server Add-on Package', containing a set of useful routines such as ICE and META indexing
- Corrections to the book contents

The WebExtra features outlined above are available free of charge (except for the charges associated with accessing the Internet and the World Wide Web). Just go to the Web site for International Thomson Computer Press. The URL is:

http://www.thomson.com/itcp.html

A service of I⟨T⟩P

The Webmaster's Handbook

Perl Power for your Web Server

Christian Neuss

Johan Vromans

INTERNATIONAL THOMSON COMPUTER PRESS
I Ⓣ P An International Thomson Publishing Company

London • Bonn • Boston • Johannesburg • Madrid • Melbourne • Mexico City • New York • Paris
Singapore • Tokyo • Toronto • Albany, NY • Belmont, CA • Cincinnati, OH • Detroit, MI

The Webmaster's Handbook
Perl Power for your Web Server

I⟨T⟩P   A division of International Thomson Publishing Inc.
          The ITP logo is a trademark under licence

British Library Cataloguing-in-Publication Data
A catalogue record for this book is available from the British Library

Library of Congress Cataloging-in-Publication Data
A catalog record for this book is available from the Library of Congress

First printed 1996

Commissioning Editor: Liz Israel Oppedijk
Cover Designed by: Button Eventures
Typeset in the Netherlands by: Squirrel Design
Printed in the UK by: Clays Ltd, St Ives plc

ISBN 1-85032-253-8

International Thomson Computer Press   International Thomson Computer Press
Berkshire House   20 Park Plaza
High Holborn   14th Floor
London WC1V 7AA   Boston MA 02116
UK   USA

http://www.thomson.com/itcp.html

Imprints of International Thomson Publishing

Contents

Foreword

I have known the authors of this useful book for a long time: at least in terms of the Internet and the Web. It has been only a few years, but it feels like a lifetime. The details of our initial encounter form a typical anecdote about the interaction between traditional society and cyberspace, but that is another story. Suffice it to say that working later on several projects with the people from IGD was a great pleasure. Their competence needs no advertizing.

In a field that seethes with activity day and night, it is no easy task to write a book. Indeed some may question the necessity for writing a book at all, given the availability of information on the Web itself. Is the book not going to be out of date overnight? I don't believe so, or at least not at this stage. This volume guides the programmer through the period following the initial setting up of a Web site, describing the techniques involved in providing a host of very useful services to his or her user community. This is no trivial task and the present book is a very helpful guide. Having the information on paper is necessary as long as we do not have pervasive networking. And then, paper or not, a comprehensive guide is certainly of great benefit to the Webmasters of the world.

This handbook is packed with complete examples, tried and tested, and available for down-loading. They are clearly explained, not too difficult to implement, useful, and above all they whet your appetite to go further.

I recommend this book to everyone wanting to set up a Web server, or indeed already running one. I hope that the authors will keep up their good work and supply us with updates as the technology evolves.

Robert Cailliau
World Wide Web support
CERN, September 1995

Preface

The World Wide Web is currently experiencing enormous popularity. While it was originally developed to provide a distributed hypermedia system for information exchange among researchers, it soon gained widespread acceptance and has been enthusiastically adopted by the international business community. Running a Web server facilitates the inexpensive distribution of information. Server software is available for all major computing platforms, and a growing number of people are becoming interested in setting up Web servers.

With the development of fill-out forms, an important new feature, interactivity, was added to the Web, thus providing user interface elements which allow for user feedback, complex search interfaces, and even transactions such as electronic registration or the sale of goods. Such Web features and functionality, by their very nature, must be customized. Features such as forms interfaces and indexing are implemented by programming customized server extensions using the *Common Gateway Interface* (CGI), which is described in Chapter 4. The creation of CGI-compliant gateways is the main theme of this book.

The Webmaster's Handbook is aimed at information-providers who want to enhance their Web server functionality and provide fill-out forms support. It contains a detailed description of Web server technology and the CGI standard for creation of information gateways. Sample code for both simple scripts and more sophisticated gateways is provided and discussed in detail. Practical tasks like creating a searchable index, conducting electronic transactions, and providing gateways to existing database management systems are discussed. All the code examples are written in the programming language Perl. Perl is often used for creating CGI interfaces, and, due to its pattern-matching capabilities and security features, it is probably the best tool for this task. Perl is also an excellent tool for processing log files and generating reports.

In this book we aim to provide a toolkit for customizing Web server functionality. The appendix contains commented source code for complete programs covering the areas outlined. All sources are also included on the CDROM supplied with this book, and will be updated regularly on the International Thomson Publishing Web site.

Acknowledgments

Several people have helped us in the writing of this book, each of them in their own special way. We would like to thank Liz Israel Oppedijk (ITP), Andrew Ford, Catherine Mason, Peter Flynn, Aileen Barry, Mark Bishop, John Martin, Tom Christiansen (Perl), Robert Cailliau (CERN) and Jos Vos (X/OS Open Systems Consultants) for their assistance.

Chris: My thanks go to my friends at IGD, especially Steffi, Trice, Ralph and Holger, for their encouragement and support. I would also like to thank the virtual community of Usenet, without whom I would never have learned of either Perl or the Web.

Johan: I specifically want to thank Heleen de Kruijff, Frank Baerveldt and my musical and personal friends from the 'Oktopedians' and the 'ACC Big Band'. I dedicate this book to our inspirational musical director Herman de Wit, who died unexpectedly a couple of months ago. He would not have understood much of this book, but music was the common language we spoke and enjoyed.

1

Introduction

The Internet is a global network that connects millions of people from all over the world, with new users and machines joining every day. Various databases and information services have long been accessible on the Internet, but until a few years ago, they were more or less hidden behind interfaces that were difficult to learn and to use. Using these systems often required learning a cryptic query language, and thus information access was in practice restricted to specialists.

The birth of the World Wide Web at CERN in 1989, along with the development of easy to use graphical browsers like NCSA's Mosaic, has given a new face to the Internet. Suddenly, an ever-increasing wealth of information was readily accessible by the simple means of clicking on a highlighted text phrase. The World Wide Web is currently undergoing an an enormous popularity boom, with a steadily growing base of servers in private, educational and corporate spheres.

Many enterprises are establishing a presence on the Internet, where they can advertise their products, publicize their business, or sell information and services. Running a Web server allows for inexpensive, instant distribution of information, which can be frequently updated whenever changes are necessary. It provides an excellent means of maintaining corporate-wide internal communication as well as a cost-effective information service for customers, and even allows orders to be placed electronically.

It is not at all difficult to set up a Web site. Web server software is available for most common platforms, including not only most flavors of Unix, but also Macintoshes and Windows NT based personal computers. However, providing the physical connection and setting up a Web server is only the first step. In order to provide enhanced server features like on-line customer response forms or searchable product databases, the Web server has to be augmented with customized functionality. A server administrator must not only be familiar with the installation and configuration of the server, but also be able to maintain things like gateway programs, forms, databases, and applications that will work together on the system.

Customizing functionality is achieved by adding external programs into the server's virtual document space. Through server-side executable programs, a Web server can produce *dynamic documents* on the fly, and wrap just about every service or information resource into a Web-compatible form. These programs can create forms and process their input, provide a gateway interface to existing information systems or databases, and provide a searchable interface to document repositories.

Our book aims to provide Webmasters and server administrators with the necessary tools and know-how for enhancing a Web server with this customized functionality. It describes in detail the underlying communication protocols and interfaces on which server gateways are based. Using the Perl programming language as a teaching medium, we analyze and discuss sample code for tasks such as handling forms input, providing searchable document repositories and creating gateways to database systems. All the code samples from the book are included on the accompanying CDROM, together with more sophisticated programs and various free tools and libraries.

1.1   The World Wide Web

The World Wide Web is a distributed, hypermedia information system, initially developed at CERN, the European Laboratory for Particle Physics near Geneva, Switzerland. The first Web server and browser software was created on a NeXT computer by Tim Berners-Lee of CERN in 1990.

The Web features a document markup language, *Hypertext Markup Language* (HTML), which has a twofold purpose: *connectivity* – documents can be connected with each other through semantic reference, using a universal naming scheme, and *interface* – the markup language specifies features far beyond linkage of documents. The Hypertext Markup Language consists of text with embedded formatting tags and hyperlinks pointing to other hypermedia documents. The hyperlink consists of the location of the information resource, and the access method required to retrieve it.

The markup language is accompanied by a naming scheme for network information resources, *Uniform Resource Locator* (URL), and a protocol for accessing and transferring documents, *Hypertext Transfer Protocol* (HTTP). As well as addressing documents hosted by Web servers, a URL can also point to information served by Gopher, WAIS, FTP or other types of server, thus the World Wide Web can integrate various information resources within a single interface.

Although the Web had a mouse-based user interface from its inception, it was originally text oriented. It was only with the release of the Mosaic browser in 1993 that the Web gained wide-spread popularity. Its most innovative feature was its ability to display images within documents. Mosaic, which was developed at the United States National Center for Supercomputing Applications (NCSA), features a fully graphical interface.

The availability of Mosaic for a variety of platforms was largely responsible for the rapid increase in popularity of the World Wide Web over the last two years. The Web is now the most popular way of accessing Internet-based information services. In fact, the phrase 'World Wide Web' is often used not only to refer to the collective network of servers, but also to the global body of information available to Web browsers.

The World Wide Web is based on a simple client–server model. The client program is known as a *Web Browser*, a program that retrieves and renders hypertext files. In order to retrieve a hypertext document, a Web client has to initiate a connection to the machine specified and request a document transfer. In order to be able to handle the request, the remote site runs a *Web Server* program. Its task is basically to wait for a browser to initiate a document request and, given that the client has the permission to retrieve the document specified, encode and pass the document back to the client. The machine running the server program is itself often called a Web server, despite the fact that it usually runs many other programs.

Servers and browsers are connected through a network (usually the Internet) using the Hypertext Transfer Protocol. The addressing scheme for locating information resources using URLs is also a fundamental part of the World Wide Web.

Hyperlinks can point to several kinds of sources of information, such as HTML documents, FTP servers and Telnet gateways. Although hyperlinks often point to static information, they can also point to information generated on demand. Web servers usually provide mechanisms for invoking external programs that dynamically generate or convert information, and for mapping these programs into the servers document space, thus providing seamless integration of other information resources.

1.2   Managing a Web site

The tasks of managing a Web site have a lot in common with the normal duties of a system administrator. They include installation and maintenance of software, overseeing system security, and helping users with problems. As well as setting up and maintaining a network connection, managing a Web site also involves:

- *Setting up and configuring the server.*
  After the server software has been installed, it needs to be configured and fine-tuned for optimum performance. Security issues must be addressed, and access schemes for non-public data set up.

- *Log file management.*
  Log files provide users and administrators with important feedback on which documents are popular. However, on a large site log files tend to grow very quickly, and thus must be truncated or archived at regular intervals. Usually, a statistics summary is generated before removing the log files and kept on-line for a longer period of time.

- *Providing usage charts.*
  Both remote users and local information-providers may be interested in statistics and usage charts, which can be automatically generated and mapped into the server's document space.

- *Setting up searchable repositories.*
  Information usually has to be prepared before it can be made accessible.

- *Running automatic consistency checkers.*
  Documents can contain hypertext links to other information and it is important to verify the correctness of these links.

- *Setting up dynamic enhancements.*
  Handling forms and interfacing to database systems and existing information services usually requires server extensions.

Most of these tasks necessitate customizing or augmenting the Web server, indeed, many of the advanced features of Web servers need to be customized in. A well-defined interface has been developed for this purpose.

1.3   Customizing the server

The basic installation and configuration of a Web server permits anyone with Internet access to retrieve the documents made available. However, it does not allow for advanced features and services of the Web such as fill-out forms or electronic catalogues. Commercial users often require specialized services which are implemented as server enhancements, often as gateway programs, for example:

- On-line ordering through fill-out forms.

- Guest books and membership questionnaires.

- Electronic catalogues with database access.

- Email interfaces.

The *Common Gateway Interface* (CGI), defines how the server and gateway programs communicate by specifying a set of environment variables. These environment variables provide the gateway program with information such as the address of the remote client, the server software version, or the parameters from a fill-out form.

Gateways programs can be used for a variety of purposes, the most common being the processing of keyword queries and evaluation of forms input. Other common uses for gateway programs include:

- Dynamic generation of statistical reports and graphics.

- Creation of a user-friendly interface to a customized search facility.

- Automatic email response forms.

- The on-demand conversion of manual pages to hypertext.

1.4   The Perl programming language

Perl is considered by most Web script programmers to be the language of choice for writing Web server gateway programs. Not only do its features make it an excellent tool for the task, there are also hundreds of existing tried and tested Perl programs available free on the Internet.

Perl is a programming language which was created for scanning text files, extracting information, and generating reports on the extracted data (in fact, the name Perl itself is an acronym for Practical Extraction and Report Language). It is also an excellent language for many system management tasks. Perl was developed by Larry Wall in the late 1980's, since when it has grown tremendously, both in language functionality and user base. Version 4 of Perl has been mature for a couple of years and is one of the most popular programs on the Internet. Version 5 of Perl, released early in 1995, includes facilities for object oriented programming and looks set to become as popular as its predecessor. Although originating in the Unix environment, Perl is now very widespread and available on most computer systems. And furthermore it is free!

The combination of text processing, report generation and system management facilities makes Perl an excellent choice for Web server management. Common server administrator tasks such as report generation and log file processing are easily handled. Perl is also well suited to the creation of server enhancements that evaluate forms data or interface to existing information systems such as relational databases.

Perl's pattern-matching and string-processing features facilitate argument parsing and manipulation. Its support for interprocess communication also makes the invoking of external programs fairly simple. Perl programs are run by the Perl compiler/interpreter, which combines the speed of interpretive program development with the efficiency of modern compilers. This makes Perl programs extremely portable.

Throughout this book, we will use Perl as a teaching medium. Its expressive power allows well written Perl programs to be compact, clear and concise. The equivalent task coded in a language such as C usually results in a program that is much longer and less easily understood. This clarity and succinctness is largely the result of Perl's built-in pattern matching capabilities and high level string operations. Of course, Perl programs can also become fairly cryptic and unreadable – as the saying goes, a Real Programmer can write Fortran programs in any language. In principle almost any programming language can be used to write gateway programs: C, Tcl, Python, Icon, Visual Basic, even shell scripts. In practice the choice of language will depend on availability and the programmer's experience.

All the examples and code fragments in this book have been tested on a Unix system under version 5 of Perl, but most of them will also work with version 4. Although initially developed under Unix, nowadays Web servers run on most major platforms, including VMS, Apple Macintosh and PCs running Microsoft Windows,

Windows NT or OS/2. Not surprisingly, Perl is also available on most of these platforms. The fundamentals of running a Web server and of Perl programming do not differ greatly between operating systems. However, if you are a running a Web server on a non-Unix platform then the examples from this book may need minor modifications before they work on your system.

2

Web Server Technology

The provision of advanced Web server features such as forms processing requires a certain amount of customizing and enhancing of the Web server. Almost all add-on functionality is implemented by external gateway programs. In the next chapters, we will show how gateways can be used to enhance Web servers, but first we need to examine the underlying Web server technology in some detail. This chapter covers client–server communication, as well as the transfer encoding of documents, and introduces the concept of creating dynamic hypertext files.

2.1 Tasks of a Web server

The main purpose of a Web server is to provide information through a well-defined access mechanism. The Web server allows clients to connect to it and request information transfers. Serving documents involves more than just sending files over a network connection. The presentation of the information (the interpretation and rendering of HTML) is left completely to the client, the server controls the storage and retrieval of documents and their transfer encoding. The Web server is also responsible for providing encryption and client authentication, and often allows for integrating dynamic documents and gateways to existing services.

Web servers perform the following tasks:

- *Provide abstract to physical path mapping.*
  Static documents are stored as files within the server's file system. Every URL represents a single file accessible by the server machine. The full physical path name of a document is often rather long and unwieldy. In order to keep URLs to a manageable length the server provides a mapping scheme that translates abstract paths in a URL to the full physical paths defining the file's location. For example, if on the server all hypertext files reside in a directory: `/disk3/usr2/documents/`, without a path translation mechanism, a URL would be:

```
http://www.some.site/disk3/usr2/documents/www/hello.html
```

By defining a mapping between a short, readable name, and the physical path where a document or directory actually resides, the same file could be accessed less tortuously as:

```
http://www.some.site/HotStuff/hello.html
```

which is both easier to type and to remember. URLs are covered more extensively in Section 2.3.1.

- *Provide protection and password evaluation.*
  In some situations it may be desirable to restrict the availability of certain documents to privileged users. This can be achieved using document protection schemes based on a variety of attributes, such as the identity of the remote host that has issued the request, or a password-based authentication mechanism.

- *Log requests and errors for later evaluation.*
  If a request fails or is denied, the server returns a message to the client indicating the reason. The server should log all requests, successful or otherwise, as document usage data can be very useful. Often, a failed document request indicates a misspelled or outdated URL in another document. The logs also yield valuable feedback on how easy it is to reach a specific document, and the relative popularity of individual documents.

- *Encode documents of different types.*
  Web browsers exist on a variety of platforms, which may have different methods of document or data representation. For instance, the byte ordering of binary files may differ, or the line break character may not be the same on server and client machines. Using a canonical format for messages and data solves this problem. The Web uses a format related to the MIME encoding mechanism for Internet mail (Section 2.3.3).

- *Provide a gateway mechanism to external routines.*
  The information requested by a client program may not always be a static file. It might be something that can only be generated at the moment the request is made, such as the number of requests currently being served. In order to allow for easy integration of dynamic information, Web servers can provide a gateway mechanism that invokes an external program and converts its output to a format that can be passed on to the client.

You may have noticed that maintaining link consistency (ensuring that every hyperlink does indeed point to something) is not listed as a server task. Current Web technology leaves this as the responsibility of the document author, but the server administrator can (and should) help with tools at least to check local links for consistency.

2.2 Information gateways

Web servers can be enhanced with customized functionality through a simple yet very powerful mechanism which defines an interface for inclusion of external routines. These are often referred to as gateway scripts, gateway programs, or CGI programs since they conform to the Common Gateway Interface standard.

A gateway is a program which processes requests for information not stored as a Web document, and generates a Web document containing the requested information. Gateway programs are invoked by the server when requested. Through the gateway mechanism, a Web server can deliver information that is not normally accessible to the client. For example, information stored inside a relational database system can normally only be accessed by means of special front-ends and database applications. By providing a gateway between the Web server and the database system, information can be converted to HTML format and thus be made available to Web clients.

Interfacing to other information resources is not the only application for gateway programs. They can be used for a variety of purposes, the most prominent of which is the processing of fill-out forms. Forms are an important part of the Web, since they provide the necessary basic mechanism for performing transactions. Since forms submission by its very nature requires customized treatment, decoding and processing the form input is handled by a gateway program.

Various kinds of dynamically generated information are available through gateway mechanisms. A server can deliver the results of a database query, or of a search in the server's document space, or even an up-to-date photograph of a coffee machine (in fact, virtual coffee machines were very popular Web demos back in 1994).

The potential of the features that can be provided through gateways is probably best illustrated by example. Figure 2.1 on the next page shows a fill-out form from the CDnow Internet Music Archive[1] which serves as a front-end to an electronic catalogue. By entering data into the form and submitting it, the catalogue can be searched for items on sale.

A successful search leads to a page similar to the one shown in Figure 2.2 on page 11. Each line in the list of search hits contains clickable icons that perform functions such as providing detailed information, or entering the item into a *virtual shopping cart*. Other form interfaces allow the user to actually purchase the items selected, by providing credit card information, or preparing an order for despatch on receipt of a money order or cheque.

All kinds of information repositories can be accessed via gateway programs, including industry standard relational database systems. Through fill-out forms, customers can be provided with an attractive and powerful user interface for accessing corporate information systems. Forms can also be used for on-line ordering of goods and services.

[1]http://cdnow.com

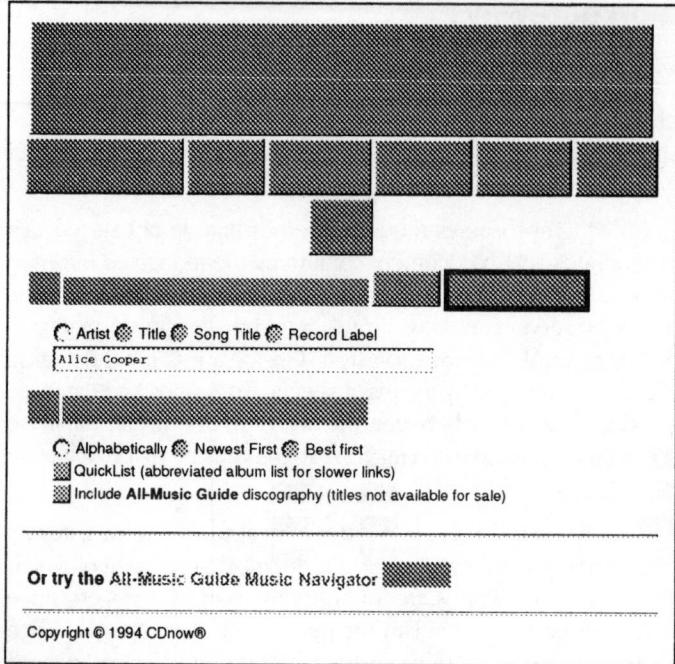

C Artist ⊗ Title ⊗ Song Title ⊗ Record Label
Alice Cooper

C Alphabetically ⊗ Newest First ⊗ Best first
QuickList (abbreviated album list for slower links)
Include **All-Music Guide** discography (titles not available for sale)

Or try the All-Music Guide Music Navigator

Copyright © 1994 CDnow®

Figure 2.1   Fill-out form for an electronic catalogue
(Courtesy of CDnow Internet Music Archive)

The Common Gateway Interface defines how Web server and external program communicate through a standardized environment. Figure 2.3 on page 12 shows the components and protocols involved in the process. All protocols will be described in more detail in the next section. The steps in this process are:

- On receiving a client request, the server sends an HTML document containing a fill-out form. This is a normal HTML document with directives that specify interface elements such as checkboxes and input fields. Client–server communication uses the HTTP protocol.

- When the user submits the form, the browser program encodes the forms data and transfers it to the server.

- The server invokes a gateway program and passes it the forms data as variables. The CGI protocol defines how information is passed from the server to the gateway program.

- Finally, after the gateway program has completed its task (for instance a database access to a catalogue), the information is transferred back to the client as an HTML document.

The following section gives a brief overview of the protocols and encoding schemes used in Web client–server communication. The standards and technology of gateway programs are discussed in subsequent chapters.

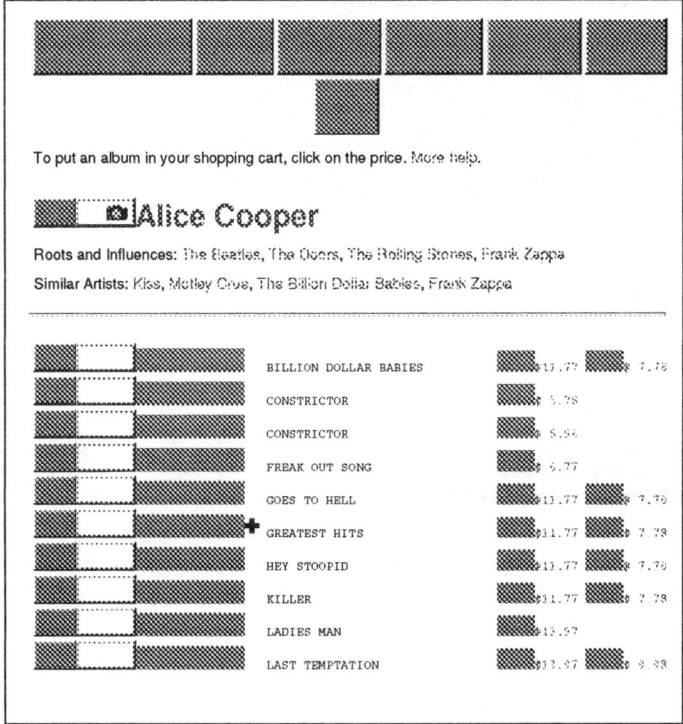

Figure 2.2   Electronic catalog: list of search hits
(Courtesy of CDnow Internet Music Archive)

2.3   Protocols and specifications

The Web became the *lingua franca* of the Internet because it was built on a set of open standards which define such things as how client and servers communicate, and the markup directives that are used in hypertext documents.

A complete definition of all protocol elements and related standards is maintained by the World Wide Web Consortium (W3C) and can be found at http://www.w3.org/. The World Wide Web Consortium is an industry consortium run by the Laboratory for Computer Science at the Massachusetts Institute of Technology (MIT). Its aim is to promote the Web by producing specifications and reference software. In Europe, MIT collaborates with CERN, the originators of the Web, and INRIA, the European W3C centre. The W3C Web server is updated frequently, and is a good source of information on protocols, standards, and the latest developments in Web technology.

This section provides an overview of the client–server communication and the addressing scheme employed by Web software. It can be used as a compact reference when writing applications.

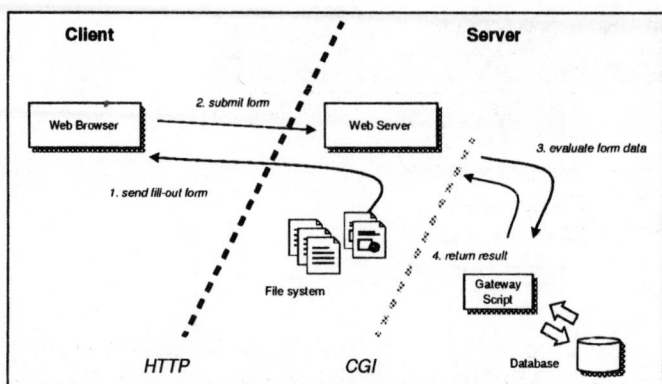

Figure 2.3 Gateway technology and protocols involved

2.3.1 Uniform Resource Locators

The World Wide Web uses a universal naming scheme, the *Uniform Resource Locator*, to specify the exact location of an information resource, and the network protocol necessary to retrieve it. The general syntax is:

> *scheme* : *path*

where *scheme* identifies the protocol, such as HTTP, Gopher or FTP required to access the resource. The interpretation of *path* depends on the protocol. In the case of the HTTP protocol it has the following syntax:

> http://*hostname* [: *port*] / *document path*

By convention, text enclosed within square brackets ('[' and ']') is optional. The *host name* is a unique reference to the remote host and is preceded by a leading double slash '//'. After the host name a *port number* may follow, separated from the host name by a colon ':'. A port is a number that supplements an Internet host address to identify a particular service. Standard Internet services such as *ftp* and *finger* are associated with fixed port numbers defined by Internet standards documents rather misleadingly termed *Requests for Comments* (RFC). On typical Unix systems a list of these port numbers can be found in the configuration file /etc/services.

After the host name and port number, the *document path* follows. It is evaluated by the server and refers to a hypermedia document in the server's name space.

Let's take a look at a simple example of a URL:

> http://www.igd.fhg.de:8001/www/www95/www95.html

It consists of three parts. The first part, http, defines the access scheme – the resource will be retrieved using the HTTP protocol. The access scheme is terminated with a colon. Table 2.1 shows a number of common schemes.

After the protocol scheme and the delimiting characters '//' the remote host is specified. It can either be given as a host name or as a number. Both formats

Table 2.1   Common URL access schemes

Scheme	Port number	Purpose
http	80	Hypertext document transfer
ftp	21	File Transfer Protocol
telnet	23	Interactive Telnet
news	119	Usenet news
mailto	25	Electronic mail
gopher	70	Internet Gopher

uniquely identify a machine on the Internet. The host name format is a string consisting of a list of names separated by dots, in our example: `www.igd.fhg.de`. It is intended to be abstract and human-readable. Using the *Domain Name System* (DNS)[2], this abstract machine name is translated to its numerical equivalent: an *IP number*[3]. In the example a port number has also been given, separated from the host name by a colon. In combination with the host name, the port number designates the server program on the target host. For the `http` scheme the default port number is 80. Using different port numbers, a host can run several Web servers simultaneously.

The final part of the URL starts with a single slash. It defines a hierarchical path of names separated by slashes. Although the URL path looks like a Unix file name, its interpretation is system independent and is left completely to the server program. Although current servers retrieve documents from the file system, in the future, documents will probably be served directly from a database system in many instances. Where this is the case, URL paths will no longer reflect a physical hierarchy of file name components.

The separation of a resource locator address into server address and document path has a very practical reason. In order to access documents in a large distributed system, an abstract addressing scheme with a hierarchical directory service had to be developed. At that time the only addressing scheme available was DNS. By splitting up document addresses into a host name and a host relative document path, the DNS service could be employed to provide a world-wide document naming scheme.

Of course this approach has some drawbacks. If a Web site changes its Internet host name (perhaps by changing its Internet access provider), all links leading to that site become invalid. Furthermore, the URL addressing scheme does not support the unique identification of documents. There is no way of telling whether two different URLs point to an identical document without retrieving both documents and comparing them. This is potentially problematic for caching and distributed repositories. A further problem arises when documents are moved. All references to

---

[2] A distributed service responsible for mapping abstract host names to IP numbers. Internals and setup of DNS are covered by the excellent book on Unix system administration by Nemeth et al [Neme95] and [Albi92].

[3] An IP number is a 32-bit numeric value, which is usually written as four decimal numbers (each encoding one byte of the IP number) separated by dots, for example `127.0.2.1`.

them become invalid. To address these issues, the *Internet Engineering Task Force* (IETF), the protocol engineering and development arm of the Internet, has formed a Working Group to define a standard for unique *Uniform Resource Identifiers* (URI)[4], which will specify information resources on the Internet in a location independent form. This will allow for the development of resource discovery and access tools that will be much more sophisticated than any currently available, although it will probably be some time before such tools are in general use.

URL encoding

The syntax of URLs[5] is formally defined in RFC 1738. Not all ASCII characters are permitted in URLs. Non-permissible characters, such as '<' and '>', and characters that have a special meaning, such as '/' and ':', must be encoded by a percent sign ('%') followed by two hexadecimal digits (0–9, A–F) giving the ordinal value for that character in the ISO 8859 character set. Table 2.2 shows a number of common encodings. Encoding and decoding is quite straightforward and is described in Section 5.2.1.

Table 2.2   Common `url` encodings

Character	Encoding
+	%2B
&	%26
=	%3D
/	%2F
~	%7E
%	%25
space	%20

2.3.2   The Hypertext Transfer Protocol

The *Hypertext Transfer Protocol* (HTTP) defines the communication between Web client and server. It has been in use by the World Wide Web since 1990. HTTP is quite simple and straightforward. It consists basically of a 'send me this file' request from a Web browser to a Web server, and a 'here it is' reply from the server (or, in the event of an error, an appropriate error message).

The Hypertext Transfer Protocol is stateless, which means that the server does not maintain any state information about the requests it processes, and therefore can not know if a particular request is related to a request it processed earlier. This makes implementing an HTTP compliant application relatively easy (one of the reasons Web software has evolved so quickly), but has drawbacks for certain tasks which require state information to be maintained across transactions. Section 7.4

---

[4]http://www.ics.uci.edu/pub/ietf/uri/
[5]http://www.w3.org/hypertext/WWW/Addressing/URL/Overview.html

discusses methods for encoding state information into URLs in order to circumvent this problem.

A client initiates a transfer by making a connection to a server and sending a request for a data item. The server responds with a status line with its protocol version and a success or error code, followed by the data itself. After the transmission is finished, the connection is closed. The elements of an HTTP request are:

- The type of request, known as a request method, to be performed on the resource identified. In order to retrieve a file from the server, the client issues a GET request. Other valid methods are: HEAD, PUT, POST, DELETE, LINK and UNLINK.

- A URL identifying the resource.

- The protocol version.

- Finally, a MIME-like message containing request modifiers, client information and body content. All these message fields are optional.

A simple example demonstrates this:

```
GET /www/www95/www95.html HTTP/1.0
Accept: text/html
Accept: image/gif
    (a blank line)
```

The blank line serves to indicate the end of the request. HTTP uses *Internet Media Types* (formerly referred to as *MIME Content-Types*) in order to allow entities to be transmitted in a wide variety of representations. Entities must be converted to canonical form before they are transferred. For instance, ASCII text files have different line break characters or character sequences on different platforms. The line break character(s) should be converted by the server to the canonical CR/LF form. If necessary, the client translates the CR/LF back to the local line break conventions.

Since clients may not understand every multi-media file format the server is capable of serving, HTTP defines an optional mechanism for content negotiation. By providing a list of accepted content types, the client can specify which formats it is capable of handling. The server is then expected to convert the data into a form the client can accept. In the example above, the client indicates that it is capable of handling HTML and GIF images.

In response to the above request, the server might reply as follows:

```
HTTP/1.0 200 OK
Date: Tuesday, 25-Apr-95 18:42:53 GMT
Server: NCSA/1.3
MIME-Version: 1.0
Content-Type: text/html
Last-Modified: Tuesday, 25-Apr-95 18:40:12 GMT
Content-Length: 1524
    (a blank line)
```

The reply indicates that the server agrees to use HTTP version 1.0, that the request has been processed successfully (status '200 OK'), that it uses MIME version 1.0, and that the returned entity is of the content type HTML. Subsequent lines contain information on the document itself: the time of last modification and the document size in bytes. Like the client request, the server response header is also terminated by a single blank line. This is followed by the document content. Table 2.3 shows the request methods defined by HTTP version 1.0. Table 2.5 on page 18 shows some common status codes. The source code for a simple HTTP server is given in Section A.5.1 and for a simple client in Section A.5.2.

Table 2.3   HTTP methods

Request	Function
GET	Retrieve the information identified by the requested URL.
HEAD	Retrieve the document meta-information but not the document itself.
PUT	Requests that the information supplied be stored under the URL specified.
POST	Provides the server with additional data relating to the URL specified.
DELETE	Requests that the server delete the resource specified.
LINK	Establishes one or more link relationships between an existing resource identified by the URL and other existing resources.
UNLINK	Removes one or more link relationships from an existing resource identified by the URL.

2.3.3   MIME types and headers

As mentioned in the previous section, the Hypertext Transfer Protocol uses MIME encoding for transferring multi-media documents over the network. MIME stands for *Multipurpose Internet Mail Extensions*. It is an Internet standard that defines how document formats other than plain ASCII text can be passed in Internet mail messages. MIME is defined in the Internet standards RFC 1521 and RFC 1522. HTTP uses MIME as the encoding mechanism for document content and to describe document meta-information, that is, information about the document.

This section lists those HTTP header fields that are commonly used (some header elements and mechanisms defined in HTTP are not implemented yet in all Web software). For a complete list consult the World Wide Web Consortium server[6].

Header fields are used to describe the encoding, content length, content type and other attributes of documents. Client and server headers are RFC 822 compliant mail headers which specify meta-information. All header fields are optional.

---
[6]http://www.w3.org/hypertext/WWW/Protocols/Overview.html

Table 2.4 Common MIME Content Types

Content-Type	File format
application/postscript	PostScript data
application/rtf	Rich text format
application/x-tex	TEX layout system source
audio/basic	Sound file
image/gif	GIF image
image/jpeg	JPEG image
image/tiff	TIFF image
image/xbm	X bitmap image
image/x-xwindowdump	X windowdump image
text/html	HTML text
video/mpeg	MPEG animation
video/quicktime	Quicktime animation

HTTP request fields

The following field types are used in HTTP requests, that is, they are sent by the client in an HTTP protocol transaction:

Accept
This field contains a semicolon-separated list of representation schemes (Content-Type meta-information values) that the browser is capable of displaying. Only encoding schemes listed may be sent in response to this request. If no Accept field is present, it is assumed that `text/plain` and `text/html` are accepted.

An asterisk may be used in place of either the second half of the Content-Type value, or both halves to denote that the client will accept any content types the server sends.

Example:

```
Accept:  */*
Accept:  audio/*
Accept:  audio/basic
```

Table 2.4 contains a description of the most common *Content-Type* meta-information values.

Accept-Encoding
This field lists the *Content-Encoding* types that are acceptable in the response, in contrast to the `Accept` field that is used to indicate which data types the browser accepts.

Example:

```
Accept-Encoding: x-compress, x-zip
```

User-Agent
This field indicates the client software that generated the request. It is included

for statistical purposes and to trace protocol violations. The first white space delimited word must be the software product name, followed by an optional slash and version designator. Other products that form part of the user agent may be given as separate words.

Example:

```
User-Agent: Mozilla/1.1N (X11; I; SunOS)
```

Referer

This optional header field specifies the document containing the link which was followed to generate the request. It allows servers to trace invalid links back to documents which contain them (an important maintenance task for server administrators). It also makes it possible to determine which documents contain valid links to a particular document. Some servers, such as NCSA's httpd version 1.4 and above, include the Referer information in their log files.

Example:

```
Referer: http://www.iihe.ac.be/hep/pp/vanesch/mypics.html
```

Authorization

If this line is present it contains authorization information. The format is extensible but has not yet been specified, except that the first word in the line identifies the authorization system used.

If-Modified-Since

This request header is used with GET method to make it conditional. If the requested document has not changed since the time specified in this field the document will not be sent, but instead a '304 Not Modified' reply will be returned.

Table 2.5 Common status codes

Code	Meaning	Code	Meaning
200	OK	400	Bad Request
201	Created	401	Unauthorized
202	Accepted	403	Forbidden
204	No Content	404	Not Found
300	Multiple Choices	500	Internal Server Error
301	Moved Permanently	501	Not Implemented
302	Moved Temporarily	502	Bad Gateway
304	Not Modified	503	Service Unavailable

HTTP response fields

In reply to a request message, the server sends a response consisting of a status message, a general header, a response header, and meta-information on the entity the request refers to.

The first line of an HTTP 1.0 response message is the status line. It consists of the protocol version followed by a numeric status code and its associated text, for example:

```
HTTP/1.0 200 OK
```

The general header contains optional fields with information relating to the response message itself. It contains the date the message was generated, an indication as to whether or not the message was forwarded (perhaps by a proxy server), a unique message identifier, and the MIME version with which the message complies.

The response header fields allow the server to pass additional information about the response. The server may, for example, indicate which authentication scheme is applicable to the requested resource, which software version it runs, or, in case of a 'Service Unavailable' condition, inform the client when to retry the last request.

The entity header fields contain meta-information about the requested resource. The most common header fields are listed below (for a complete list, consult the HTTP/1.0 draft). If a client needs only the document meta-information, this can be retrieved using a HEAD request.

Allow

The Allow header field lists the set of methods supported for the resource identified by the HTTP request. This field informs the client of the valid methods associated with a resource and is generated in a response to a request specifying a prohibited method (status code '405 Method Not Allowed').

Example:

```
Allow: GET, HEAD, PUT
```

Content-Encoding

The Content-Encoding header field indicates how the resource has been encoded and therefore which decoding mechanism must be applied in order to obtain the unencoded media-type referenced by the Content-Type field. It is most commonly used to specify a compression scheme without losing the information about the original content type.

Example:

```
Content-Encoding: x-compress
```

In this example the client must use an appropriate decompression utility on the data to obtain the original data type defined in the Content-Type field.

Content-Length

The Content-Length header field indicates the size of the resource sent to the client, or in the case of a HEAD method, it contains the length of the resource described by the meta-information.

Example:

```
Content-Length: 3495
```

Content-Type

The Content-Type header field indicates the media type of the resource. Common values for this field are listed in Figure 2.4.

Example:

```
Content-Type: text/html; charset=ISO-8859-4
```

Expires

The Expires field gives the date and time up to which the information can be considered valid. Caching clients, including proxies, must not cache a copy of the resource beyond the date given without first re-checking its validity.

Example:

```
Expires: Thu, 01 Dec 1994 16:00:00 GMT
```

Last-Modified

This field indicates the date and time the resource was last modified. This information is useful for caching clients and can be retrieved with a HEAD request. If the client has a copy of the resource that is older than the date given in this field, the copy is out of date and the client should retrieve an up-to-date copy.

Example:

```
Last-Modified: Tue, 15 Nov 1994 12:45:26 GMT
```

Title

The Title header field contains the title of the resource as specified by the HTML <TITLE> element. This is usually the name of the document.

Example:

```
Title: Hypertext Transfer Protocol - HTTP/1.0
```

3

Dynamic Documents and Requests

The ease with which most Web servers can be extended adds considerably to their power and flexibility. Advanced features can be added not only by modifying the server sources and re-compiling, but more easily by means of external programs. These programs, traditionally called *gateway scripts* or *gateway programs* are independent of the server and can be written in almost any programming language. Their output usually comprises dynamically produced HTML documents. Information is passed between the Web server and the gateway programs using the Common Gateway Interface protocol which is described in the next chapter. This chapter explains what dynamic documents are, what their uses are, and how the CGI standard is used to create an interface to external programs from a Web server.

3.1   Dynamic documents

Most document requests can be fulfilled by returning a hypertext document stored on the server system as an ordinary file, but some situations require a more powerful mechanism. Dynamic documents are HTML documents generated by a gateway program. For example, in order to serve information not directly accessible to the client, such as the contents of an SQL database, a gateway must be set up to retrieve data from the database system and convert it into a formatted HTML document. The gateway approach is often used to cope with volatile information, which necessitates the dynamic generation of hypertext documents.

HTML lends itself to the automatic generation of documents. HTML documents are essentially streams of free-formatted information, their presentation is handled exclusively by the browser, hence document generating programs can largely ignore the task of formatting the information.

Common uses for dynamic documents include:

- Access to information that is available on the server system, but not in a suitable format, such as the Unix on-line manual pages. As it is not usually considered desirable to convert all of them to HTML format, conversion is often performed on request.

- Access to information that is on the system, but not directly available for security reasons, such as data residing in a corporate relational database system, only some of which may be retrieved.

- Access to information from certain databases, for example WAIS and Archie databases, that is only accessible through special programs. A gateway program is required to perform the necessary interfacing.

- The provision of a secure interface to potentially insecure system services, such as the *finger* program, which are often not provided directly.

- To include in a document the number of times it has been requested from the server.

Output from gateway programs is not restricted to HTML documents. Other resources such as images may also be generated.

Most modern servers and browsers use caching to improve performance and decrease the load on the network. Obviously caching tends to be incompatible with dynamic documents so caching servers usually do not cache such documents.

3.1.1   Example: counting accesses

The following example is a gateway program that generates a document showing the number of times it was accessed. Although this is a working example, it does not handle error situations and lacks facilities for concurrent access of the file that contains the current tally. These aspects are covered in later chapters.

```perl
1   #!/usr/local/bin/perl
2
3   ############### Common stuff ###############
4
5   $spooldir = '/var/spool/webmaster';
6   $tf = $spooldir . '/.tally';
7
8   ############### The Process ###############
9
10  # Emit Content-type header.
11  print STDOUT <<EOD;
12  Content-type: text/html
13
14  EOD
15
16  # Emit document header and title.
17  print STDOUT <<EOD;
18  <html> <head>
19  <title>Webmasters Handbook Example</title>
20  </head>
21  <body>
```

```
22   <h1>Webmasters Handbook Example</h1>
23   <hr>
24   EOD
25
26   # Open the tally file, and get the current count.
27   unless ( open (F, $tf) ) {
28       print STDOUT ("$tf: $!\n");
29   }
30   else {
31       $buf = <F>;
32       close (F);
33
34       # Increment it.
35       chop ($buf);
36       $tally = $buf;
37       $tally++;
38
39       # Write the new count to the tally file.
40       open (F, '>' . $tf);
41       print F ("$tally\n");
42       close (F);
43
44       # Present it to the caller.
45       print STDOUT ('You are number ', $tally,
46                     ' to visit this document.', "\n");
47   }
48
49   # Emit document trailer.
50   print STDOUT <<EOD;
51   <hr>
52   </body> </html>
53   EOD
```

3.2   Dynamic requests

With dynamic requests the user moves away from the passive selection of pre-defined choices. He or she can request the browser program to pass additional information to the Web server, for example keywords to search on. Since the server can not know beforehand which keywords will be supplied, it passes the information to a gateway program which extracts the keywords from the request and performs the desired search. Upon completion, the gateway program generates an HTML document containing the search results and passes it to the server which, in turn, sends it to the browser program.

There are currently three ways in which a user can pass additional information to a Web server: keyword queries, image maps and fill-out forms.

3.3   Keyword queries

Keyword queries were the first type of dynamic request to be implemented on the Web. If the HTML ISINDEX element is included in a document, the browser will present the user with a dialogue as shown in Figure 3.1. When keywords are entered and the data is submitted the keywords are appended, preceded by a

> This is a searchable index. Please enter search keywords: [....................................]

Figure 3.1   Typical dialogue from an ISINDEX document

question mark, to the original URL of the document to form a modified URL that is passed as a request back to the server.

Keyword queries are rather limited, usually comprising just a couple of words, and the designer of the HTML document has no control over the wording or presentation of the prompt – this is completely browser defined. Furthermore the initial URL must always point to a gateway program since this is what the server will invoke when the modified URL is returned with the query string appended.

3.4   Sensitive images

A sensitive image, or image map, is an image on which the user can click with a mouse or other pointing device, the result varying according to the position selected. The coordinates of the position selected are passed to a program whose URL is specified in the document. The coordinates are expressed in pixels counting from the lower-left corner of the picture. It is the program's task to map the coordinates to the appropriate URL.

A beautiful example of an image map is http://www.ijs.si/slo-map.html.

Newer versions of HTML provide *scribble-on images*, which are fill-out forms elements with similar functionality to that of image maps. Further information about scribble-on images is contained in Section 3.5.1.

3.5   Fill-out forms

Fill-out forms provide a powerful interactive tool on the Web: the primary means whereby the user can supply information to be passed to the server. They are used as order forms, questionnaires, data entry interfaces, query interfaces and so on.

Fill-out forms can be included in HTML documents by means of specific markup directives which define the form. The HTML FORM element designates the fill-out form within a document. This will contain INPUT, SELECT and TEXTAREA elements to specify the fields of the form that are to receive user input. When the user submits the form, having filled it out, the browser sends the data entered to the server, which passes it to the program indicated by the URL specified in the form.

The presentation and implementation of fill-out forms are determined by the browser, which uses the specific features of the operating system under which it runs. Thus, with a reasonably sophisticated graphical user interface, it is possible to present queries in the form of text fields, scrollable text fields, radio buttons and so on.

3.5.1   Interface elements

A FORM element must be entered in the body of the HTML document to create a fill-out form. The format of a FORM element is

      `<FORM` *attributes*`>` ... `</FORM>`

Multiple FORM entities in a single HTML document are permitted, but FORM entities may not be nested.

Valid attributes for the FORM element are:[1]

ACTION

    The ACTION attribute specifies the URL to which the data entered in the form should be passed. This usually points to a gateway program that will process the data.

    On typical Web servers, gateway programs and normal HTML documents reside in separate locations. In the server configuration, the directories that contain the programs are registered explicitly. When a URL refers to a document in such a directory, the server recognizes that it has to execute a program instead of just retrieving a document.

METHOD

    This defines the method used to pass the data to the ACTION URL. Two methods are supported: GET and POST. These are described more fully in Chapter 4.

ENCTYPE

    This attribute can be used to specify how the form data should be encoded when transmitted.
    The default value is `application/x-www-form-urlencoded`.

SCRIPT

    This can be used to designate scripts that are downloaded by the client and handled locally. These scripts can be used to add more control over the way the client presents the data and responds to mouse movements, clicks, pressing a key etc. Scripts can expand the capabilities of a browser, making it more than just a Web navigation tool. Do not confuse these scripts with the gateway scripts, which are the main subject of this book. The former augment the client program, the latter, the Web server.

Plain and preformatted text, lists, tables and so on can be placed within FORM elements, interspersed with special elements called *input fields*.

---

[1]This is based on the current draft specifications for HTML 3.0. The final version may differ from this draft.

The general format of most input fields is:

```
<INPUT NAME=name TYPE=type ...other attributes...>
```

The NAME attribute is mandatory. It specifies the name of the input field and is used to identify the data when transmitted to the server. The TYPE attribute is optional and specifies the type of input field. If omitted, a simple text input field is assumed. Other attributes can be added depending on the kind of input field. Note that there is no end tag (</INPUT>).

When the contents of the form are submitted to the server the information is passed as a series of name–value pairs, separated by ampersands ('&'), for example: field1=value1&field2=value2.

HTML 3.0 supports the following input fields:[2]

Simple text fields

This is the default field type, which is assumed when no TYPE attribute is specified. Any characters may be entered in this type of field. Simple text fields are used to input short text items, such as names or keywords.

Additional attributes: SIZE, a number that specifies the width of the input field as displayed by the browser. It does not, however, restrict the number of characters that may be entered. MAXLENGTH, also a number, can be used to limit the number of characters that may be entered. A default initial value can be specified with the VALUE attribute.

Example:

```
<INPUT NAME="text-field" SIZE=40>
```

Password fields

This is like a simple text field, except that the browser does not display the characters entered (often the characters appear as asterisks). Its TYPE attribute is password.

Example:

```
<INPUT NAME="password-field" TYPE=password SIZE=20>
```

Range controls

A range control can be used to impose a check on the upper and lower bounds of numeric values entered.

Example:

```
<INPUT NAME="range-field" TYPE=range MIN=1 MAX=10 VALUE=5>
```

Checkboxes

A checkbox is an input field that can have one of only two possible states: selected or not selected. Checkboxes enable the user to choose one or more alternatives out of a series of possible choices. If the checkbox is selected the value associated with it is returned to the server, otherwise nothing is returned. By default the checkbox is not selected unless the CHECKED attribute is specified, as in the following example:

---

[2]See previous footnote.

```
<INPUT NAME="check" TYPE=checkbox VALUE="Yes, I do" CHECKED>
```

This displays only the checkbox – accompanying text is needed to tell the user what the checkbox is for.

Radio buttons

Radio button input fields follow the familiar model, whereby only one of a set of radio buttons may be selected at any one time.

Example:

```
<INPUT NAME="radiobutton"  TYPE=radio VALUE="Red" CHECKED>
<INPUT NAME="radiobutton"  TYPE=radio VALUE="Green">
<INPUT NAME="radiobutton"  TYPE=radio VALUE="Blue">
```

Since all have the same NAME attribute, they constitute a single group of radio buttons. In the example, the first button has the CHECKED attribute, which means that its value is set to be delivered when the form is submitted. Of course, the user can select a different value by pressing one of the other buttons. As with checkboxes, additional text is needed to show the purpose of radio buttons. Radio buttons are useful to choose one alternative out of a series of possible choices.

Scribble on image

The image specified by the SRC attribute is displayed by the client and the user can scribble on top of it using a mouse or other suitable pointing device. The VALUE attribute is optional and is only used when the client cannot display the image. In this case the input field is treated as a simple text field.

Example:

```
<INPUT NAME=name TYPE=scribble SRC=url VALUE=init>
```

File widgets

A file input field allows the user to select a file from the local system, the browser displaying a file selection box for the user to make a selection. The contents of the selected file are attached to the form data when submitted. The types of file permitted can be limited with the optional ACCEPT attribute. Its value should be a comma separated list of MIME content types, such as text/*.

Example:

```
<INPUT NAME=name TYPE=file ACCEPT=mime-types>
```

Submit buttons

When selected, the submit button causes the current contents of the form to be sent to the server.

The VALUE attribute can be used to designate the text to be displayed on the button. If is it omitted the button will have a client-defined label, such as Submit Query.

The SRC attribute can be used to specify a URL for an image to be used as a graphical label for the button.

The submit button itself will not generate any data for the server unless a NAME attribute has been specified. This can be used to provide multiple submit buttons and inform the receiving program which one was selected.

Example:

```
<INPUT TYPE=submit>
```

Image fields

An image field is essentially an enhanced graphical submit button. When activated the form is submitted, as are the coordinates of the position on the image where the user clicked. The coordinates are sent as the value of the image field.

Example:

```
<INPUT NAME=name TYPE=image SRC=url>
```

Reset buttons

A reset button causes all form fields to be reset to their initial values.

Format:

```
<INPUT TYPE=reset>
```

Hidden fields

Hidden fields can be used to pass information to the server without displaying anything to the user. This can be necessary for complex transactions when state information must be kept. Hidden fields can be used to embed information in the form for transmission unmodified to the gateway program to determine its course of action, enabling several different forms to be handled by a single gateway program.

Example:

```
<INPUT NAME=name TYPE=hidden VALUE=value>
```

Multi-line text fields

Multi-line text fields allow for lengthy text input, and are elements in their own right, not a type of INPUT element.

The ROWS and COLS attributes specify the dimensions of the text area. As with simple text fields, the dimensions do not restrict the amount of text that may be entered, but merely control the size of the field, as displayed.

Default text can be included between the start and end TEXTAREA tags. The contents is always transmitted as one single string of text characters. Line breaks are transmitted as URL-encoded pairs of ASCII carriage return and linefeed characters ('%0D%0A').

Example:

```
<TEXTAREA NAME="textarea-field" ROWS=4 COLS=40>
This is the initial contents of
the the text area.
</TEXTAREA>
```

Selection boxes

Browsers usually implement selection boxes as pull down menus. The menu options are specified as a series of OPTION elements contained between the start and end SELECT tags. Only one option may be selected unless the MULTIPLE attribute is specified.

The value of each option defaults to the text following the OPTION element or may be specified using the VALUE attribute. Options can be marked as selected by including the SELECTED attribute.

Example:

```
<SELECT NAME="options-field" MULTIPLE>
<OPTION VALUE="Y" SELECTED>Yellow
<OPTION VALUE="M">Magenta
<OPTION>Cyan
</SELECT>
```

A number of other attributes can be specified for the FORM, INPUT, TEXTAREA, SELECT and OPTION elements. For further detail see the World Wide Web Consortium server[3].

---

[3] http://www.w3.org/hypertext/WWW/MarkUp/MarkUp.html

4

The CGI Specification

The *Common Gateway Interface* (CGI) is an interface definition for running external programs under an information server. It defines how server and gateway program communicate, and specifies how to exchange information using environment variables, command line arguments, and input and output streams.

Gateways conforming to the CGI specification can be written in any programming or scripting language, if the language can produce an executable program that is capable of exchanging information as specified above. Some of the more popular languages used for gateway programs include Perl, Tcl, the Bourne and C shells, and C/C++.

There are two methods for passing information to a gateway program, named after the HTTP commands that are used to call the gateway program: GET and POST. Most gateway programs usually handle either GET or POST input, although it is possible to design the program to handle both.

Figure 2.3 on page 12 shows the relationship between a Web server, the browser and a gateway program.

The basic sequence of events is as follows:

1. The server sends an HTML document, for example a fill-out form, as requested by the browser.

2. When the user hits the submit button, the browser submits the data to the server using the POST or GET method.

3. The server recognizes that the URL points to a gateway program, and passes the information to it. The recognition mechanism is described below.

4. The gateway program processes the information and returns a new HTML document to the server which passes the document to the browser for presentation to the user.

How does the Web server know that a URL designates a gateway program instead of a normal document? In the server configuration one or more document paths are defined as *exec paths*. URLs that start with one of these paths are always considered gateway programs, resulting in the named file being executed as a program rather than being sent back to the client.

How exec paths are specified depends on the Web server in use. Assuming that the path /htbin/ is defined to be an exec path, then the URL /htbin/pgm designates the gateway program pgm in this directory. Items following the program name in the URL are passed as additional information in an environment variable, thus /htbin/foo/bar does not designate a program foo/bar, but just foo, with /bar passed as additional information. This technique is further described in Section 6.4.2.

4.1   The GET method

The GET method is so called because the browser uses the HTTP GET command to submit query data, passing the data in the URL.

Consider an HTML document http://www.master.web/htbin/ixdemo that allows for a keyword query. When the user enters a keyword and submits the query, a new URL is formed by appending the keyword to the original URL, resulting in a new URL http://www.master.web/htbin/ixdemo?keyword. The client opens a connection to the server, and issues the command:

```
GET /htbin/ixdemo?keyword HTTP/1.0
```

The server recognizes that bin/ixdemo is a gateway program, and executes it, passing the query string keyword as a command line argument.

Since the data the user has entered can contain arbitrary characters, URL-encoding as described in Section 2.3.1, must be used.

In the early days of fill-out forms, the GET command was used to collect the request data. Since a fill-out form can contain several fields with information, the URLs can easily become very long, for example:

```
http://www.master.web/htbin/formdemo?name=john&occupation=webmaster
```

Many Web servers place an upper limit on the length of URLs, therefore a new method to pass the request data was defined, the POST method, described below.

Note that only query strings resulting from keyword queries are passed via the command line. All other query information is passed using environment variables as described in Section 4.3.

4.2   The POST method

The POST method differs from the GET method in an important aspect: the information is not passed via the URL and the command line, but via the input and output channels of the programs involved. This allows for virtually unlimited amounts of data to be passed and avoids problems with 'difficult' characters. For these reasons it is the preferred method of transferring forms data.

To issue a POST command, the client opens a connection to the server and sends a POST command. The forms data is then sent through the connection. The length of the input data is passed to the gateway program in an environment variable and the end of the data is not signaled by a terminator or end-of-file condition.

The data sent is URL-encoded to avoid misinterpretation. The string 'xx=yy=zz' could be interpreted as meaning that the field 'xx' contains the value 'yy=zz' or that the field 'xx=yy' contains the value 'zz'. Encoding solves this ambiguity: the first case would be encoded 'xx=yy%3Dzz', and the second case as 'xx%3Dyy=zz'. Gateway programs must apply URL-decoding to the data obtained via the POST method.

4.3   Environment variables

When the server runs the gateway program it creates a number of environment variables with information for the gateway to use.

The current CGI specification, version 1.1[1], lists the following variables:

SERVER_SOFTWARE
 The name and version of the server software, for example CERN/3.0.

SERVER_NAME
 The server's host name or alias, or its IP address. This can be used to create self-referencing URLs.

GATEWAY_INTERFACE
 The revision of the CGI specification to which this server complies, for example CGI/1.1.

SERVER_PROTOCOL
 The name and revision of the information protocol of the request, for example HTTP/1.0.

SERVER_PORT
 The port number to which the request was sent, usually 80, the standard port for HTTP servers.

REQUEST_METHOD
 The method by which the request was made – GET or POST.

PATH_INFO
 Information in the the URL following the part that identifies the gateway program. This information is URL-decoded.

---

[1]http://hoohoo.ncsa.uiuc.edu/cgi/

PATH_TRANSLATED

The server maintains a series of mapping rules to map logical paths to file names. The variable PATH_TRANSLATED contains the expanded information from PATH_INFO after applying these mappings. For example, if the document root (/) is mapped by the server to the directory /var/htdocs and a gateway program is called using the URL /htbin/formdemo/more, PATH_INFO contains /more and PATH_TRANSLATED contains /var/htdocs/more.

SCRIPT_NAME

The URL of the program being executed, for example /htbin/formdemo.

QUERY_STRING

The query information (that is, the string following the question mark) in the URL that referenced this program. This information is not URL-decoded. Gateway programs should extract the query information from this variable rather than from the command line arguments.

REMOTE_HOST

The name of the remote host making the request. If this information is not available to the server the variable will not be set and the gateway program should use REMOTE_ADDR instead.

REMOTE_ADDR

The numeric IP address of the host making the request.

AUTH_TYPE

If the server supports user authentication and the program is protected, this variable contains the protocol-specific authentication method used.

REMOTE_USER

In the case of user authentication, this is the name with which the user was authenticated.

REMOTE_IDENT

The remote user name, if both server and remote system support RFC 931 identification. This variable is often not set, and even when set the value is not verifiable.

CONTENT_TYPE

This variable specifies the type of the data attached as a MIME type. It is only used with PUT and POST methods.

CONTENT_LENGTH

The length in octets of the data that is attached. It is only used with PUT and POST methods. A gateway program must use this value to determine how much data is available.

HTTP header lines passed by the client to the server may also be available in environment variables, the names of which are formed by prefixing the header name with the string 'HTTP_'. Lower case characters are converted to upper case and hyphens are replaced with underscore characters. These environment variables must be considered optional. The server usually excludes headers that are already processed, such as Content-length, and is free to exclude others.

4.4 Summary

From the point of view of a gateway program, the request data can be passed in three ways:

- *As command line arguments.*
  This is the case if the data originates from an ISINDEX or ISMAP request.

- *In the environment variable QUERY_STRING.*
  This is the case for all GET requests (including ISINDEX and ISMAP requests).

- *On the standard input stream.*
  This is the case for all POST requests. The length of data supplied is specified in the CONTENT_LENGTH environment variable.

5

Writing Gateway Programs

Before starting to construct a real gateway program from scratch, we should summarize the tasks it has to accomplish.

- The request information must be gathered from the appropriate input source.

- The request information must be processed, which usually involves consulting local files. Sending email messages and updating local databases are also common tasks for gateway programs.

- The results must be passed back to the requesting client in the form of an HTML document.

This may seem straightforward, but there are constraints:

- The gateway program runs as a stand-alone process in a fairly unsophisticated environment. There is no controlling terminal and it usually runs under a user ID that allows only limited access to most parts of the system.

- The program must be capable of retrieving the user information from the command line, from environment variables or from the standard input, and it must have a method of determining the correct input source.

- Whatever the program writes to its standard output is interpreted by the server and usually passed back to the browser, so a valid HTML document must always be generated.

One of the interesting things a gateway program can do is generate an HTML document containing a form that specifies its own URL in the ACTION attribute. Consider the following approach:

1. The browser issues a GET request to the server, passing it a URL that designates a gateway program.

2. The program is invoked by the server. Since there was no user data passed, it generates a form specifying its own URL in the ACTION attribute. The server sends this to the browser.

3. The user fills in the form and submits it. Once again, the gateway program is invoked but this time it recognizes the presence of user data and acts upon it.

A well-written gateway program should demonstrate flexibility in how it accepts data input, recognizing GET and POST methods, command line arguments and standard input data. In this chapter we demonstrate how this can be achieved.

5.1   A minimal gateway program

Our first example shows a gateway program, isixecho.pl, that responds to an ISINDEX query. In the case of an ISINDEX query, the query information is passed to the gateway program via the command line. The program is quite short, as no special processing is required:

```
 1  #!/usr/local/bin/perl
 2
 3  # First, the Contents-Type header.
 4  print STDOUT ('Content-Type: text/html', "\n\n");
 5
 6  # And a header.
 7  print STDOUT ('<h1>Echo ISINDEX query</h1>', "\n");
 8
 9  if ( @ARGV > 0 ) {
10      # There was information supplied.
11      print STDOUT ('Keywords passed:', "\n");
12
13      # Make a list of the keywords.
14      print STDOUT ('<ul>', "\n");
15      foreach $keyword ( @ARGV ) {
16          print STDOUT ('<li>', $keyword, "\n");
17      }
18      print STDOUT ('</ul>', "\n");
19  }
20
21  # Turn it into a <ISINDEX> document.
22  print STDOUT ('<isindex>', "\n");
```

For the sake of simplicity the program does not output HTML elements such as <HEAD> and <BODY>. To test the program, it can be run manually with the following command:

```
perl isixecho.pl key1 key2
```

If the program runs successfully, it can be installed in a location that the Web server is configured to recognize as containing executable programs. Assuming the server's exec path is /usr/local/lib/webmaster/cgi-bin, install the program in this directory under the name isixecho and mark it as executable (consult your system documentation on how to do this).

The program can now be tested with a browser, invoked using the URL http://localhost/cgi-bin/isixecho.

5.2   Common tasks

A number of tasks are common to almost all gateway programs. In this section we describe the most essential tasks and present Perl subroutines to carry them out. These routines are used frequently in the sample programs.

5.2.1   URL encoding and decoding

The information passed to a gateway program is encoded using the simple encoding technique previously described in Section 2.3.1.

```
1    # Subroutines to handle basic encoding/decoding of URL data.
2
3    sub url_encode {
4        local ($s) = @_;
5
6        # Translate special characters to %XX, and space to + .
7        # As documented, + < > % " / and ? are encoded since they are
8        # not allowed in URLs.
9        # Also encoded are = and & since they have special meaning
10       # in data resulting from forms input.
11       $s =~ s|([+<>%"/?=&])|sprintf("%%%02X",ord($1))|ge;
12       $s =~ tr/ /+/;
13       $s;
14   }
15
16   sub url_decode {
17       local ($s) = @_;
18
19       # Translate + to space, and %XX to the character code.
20
21       $s =~ tr/+/ /;
22       $s =~ s/%([0-9A-F][0-9A-F])/pack("C",oct("0x$1"))/ge;
23       $s;
24   }
```

The routine url_encode encodes every occurrence of the characters + < > % " / and ? into a pair of hexadecimal codes. The routine url_decode decodes *any* pair of hexadecimal codes preceded by a percent sign. This is considered correct behavior, following the Internet adage, 'be conservative with what you generate, but liberal with what you accept'.

5.2.2   Parsing the CGI environment

The server sets up a collection of environment variables for the gateway program to use, as described in Section 4.3. Probably the most important variable is QUERY_STRING, since it contains user specified information that was appended to the URL. In the example from Section 5.1, QUERY_STRING contains the URL-encoded version of the keyword information. Some examples are shown in Table 5.1.

In the case of a FORM query, QUERY_STRING contains the URL-encoded name–value pairs. Some examples are shown in Table 5.2.

Table 5.1   Example QUERY_STRING for keyword queries

Keywords	QUERY_STRING
web	web
web master	web+master
web+www master	web%2Bwww+master

Table 5.2   Example QUERY_STRING for form queries

Name1	Name2	QUERY_STRING
web		Name1=web
web	master	Name1=web&Name2=master
www=web	master	Name1=www%3Dweb&Name2=master

A convenient way to deal with the contents of the QUERY_STRING is to decode it into an associative array where the value of each name–value pair is stored using the name as the key. The following Perl code defines a routine cgiparse that parses the contents of QUERY_STRING and returns an associative array.

```
 1   # Subroutine cgiparse parses the contents
 2   # of a CGI query into an associative array.
 3   #
 4   # Typical use:
 5   #
 6   #     %query = &cgiparse();
 7   #     if ( defined $query{'Name'} ) ....
 8   #
 9   # A string of data may be passed as a parameter. This is useful
10   # for testing and for occasions where the CGI input has already
11   # been collected.
12
13   sub cgiparse {
14
15       local ($data) = @_;
16
17       # Fetch the data for this request.
18
19       if ( defined $data ) {
20           # We have data passed.
21       }
22       elsif ( $ENV{'REQUEST_METHOD'} eq 'POST' ) {
23           # Read it from standard input.
24           local ($len) = $ENV{'CONTENT_LENGTH'};
25           if ( read (STDIN, $data, $len) != $len ) {
26               die ("Error reading 'POST' data\n");
27           }
28       }
29       else {
30           # Fetch from environment variable.
31           $data = $ENV{'QUERY_STRING'};
32       }
33
34       local (%qs) = ();              # resultant hash array
35
36       # The data is encoded as name1=val1&name2=val2&etc.
37       # First split on name/value pairs.
38       foreach $qs ( split ('&', $data) ) {
39           # Then split name and value.
40           local ($name, $val) = split ('=', $qs);
41           # URL decode and put in resultant hash array.
42           $name = &url_decode ($name);
```

```
43          if ( defined $qs{$name} ) {
44              # Multiple values. Append using \0 separator.
45              $qs{$name} .= "\0" . &url_decode ($val);
46          }
47          else {
48              # Store it.
49              $qs{$name} = &url_decode ($val);
50          }
51      }
52
53      # And return it.
54      %qs;
55  }
```

At line 19 the routine checks whether it has been passed any parameter data. It then uses the environment variable REQUEST_METHOD to select the source of the query information (line 22). Splitting the data and decoding it is straightforward. Multiple values for the same name are handled by concatenating them using a NUL character as a separator (line 45).

5.2.3   Generating the HTML document

Gateway programs should always output an HTML document, even in error situations, in order to generate a meaningful response for the user. If this is not done the user may be faced with a blank screen, which can be disconcerting.

The following routines are useful in generating HTML documents.

```
1   # Print the document header.
2   sub send_header {
3       local ($type) = (@_);
4
5       # Use a suitable default.
6       if ( !(defined $type) || $type eq "" ) {
7           $type = 'text/html';
8       }
9
10      print STDOUT ("Content-Type: ", $type, "\n\n");
11  }
12
13  # Print the HTML header ...
14  sub html_start {
15      local ($title) = (@_);
16      print STDOUT ("<HTML><HEAD>\n",
17                     "<TITLE>", $title, "</TITLE>\n",
18                     "</HEAD>\n",
19                     "<BODY>\n",
20                     "<H1>$title</H1>\n");
21  }
22
23  # ... and the trailer.
24  sub html_end {
25      print STDOUT ("</BODY></HTML>\n");
26  }
```

The routine send_header outputs the Content-Type header. It takes a single optional argument, the content-type, which defaults to text/html.

The routine html_start outputs the standard HTML elements that start a document. It takes one mandatory parameter, the title of the document.

The routine html_end outputs the standard HTML elements that end a document.

5.2.4   Concurrent file access

A Web server usually handles requests by spawning a copy of itself as a separate process. The advantage of this approach is that the server does not have to wait for the current request to be completed before serving the next request. There can, however, be situations when this behavior leads to unexpected results.

Consider a simple example. In order to set up a 'virtual guest book' service, a gateway program is needed that allows users to enter their name and home page in a fill-out form. When the form is submitted, the data is appended to a guest book file on the server system. A straightforward approach might be:

1. Decode the forms data.

2. Open the guest book file for appending.

3. Write the data to the file.

4. Close the guest book file.

Difficulties may arise if two separate requests to access the guest book program are received simultaneously. The two requests are handled by separate but concurrent processes. It may happen that the second process opens the guest book file at a point in time when the first process has already opened the file but not yet appended any data. Both processes now have the guest book file open at exactly the same position and no matter which process writes its data first, an undesirable result will ensue, namely that both processes will write to the same position in the guest book file, causing data to be overwritten or corrupted. This situation, where two or more processes read or write some shared data and the final result depends on the order in which the processes perform some action, is known as a *race condition*. In general, having more than one process write to a file without adding some kind of concurrency control is bound to produce inconsistencies.

Most gateway programs only need to append a couple of lines of information to a file, so the race condition can be avoided by the simple expedient of making the file access exclusive so that only one process at a time can modify it. Once the desired updates have been made the exclusive access to the file is released. If the update can be performed in a short period of time it is often sufficient for competing processes simply to wait until the file becomes available again. This method is called *file locking*.

The following Perl code defines a subroutine `lockfile` to handle file locking using the Unix `flock` system call. In Section A.7 you will find an equivalent subroutine implemented using the `fcntl` system call.

```
1    # Subroutine lockfile:
2    #
3    #       &lockfile (FH)
4    #
5    #       FH is a handle to an opened file, with r/w access.
6    #
7    # Return values:
8    #       1   lock succeeded
```

```
 9  #     0  lock failed
10  #
11  # Locking is implemented using the flock(2) system call that is
12  # available on most modern systems.
13  #
14  # Typical use:
15  #
16  #    open (F, "+>>datafile") || die (...);
17  #    if ( &lockfile (F) ) {
18  #       seek (F, 0, 2);      # seek to end
19  #       print F (...);       # append info
20  #    }
21  #    close (F);              # release the file and lock
22
23  sub lockfile {
24      local ($FH) = @_;
25
26      local ($LOCK_SH) = 1;        # shared lock
27      local ($LOCK_EX) = 2;        # lock exclusive
28      local ($LOCK_NB) = 4;        # don't block when locking
29      local ($LOCK_UN) = 8;        # release the lock
30
31      flock ($FH, $LOCK_EX);       # lock exclusive,
32                                   # return TRUE upon success.
33  }
```

In lines 26–29 we have included all possible values for the flock system call, although only $LOCK_EX is needed. The routine's return value is true if the file was successfully locked. Since closing the file implicitly releases the lock there is no real need for a subroutine to unlock the file.

Note that this method of locking does *not* work on files, which are accessed over networking file systems like NFS. Special locking methods exist for this purpose, such as the locking tool provided by the *procmail* package[1], but these are really beyond the scope of this book.

There is more information on locking and concurrency control in Section 7.2. If you are unfamiliar with the principles of multitasking and concurrent processes and wish to learn more, we recommend Andrew Tanenbaum's book on operating systems [Tane87].

5.2.5 Date conversion

Unix systems keep track of the time by counting seconds since January 1st, 1970. Other systems have their own peculiar ways of recording time and dates. It is frequently necessary to convert these internal formats to readable or otherwise useful formats. Although there is virtually no limit to the number of possible conversions, we will define subroutines for two common cases here.

The subroutine timetostr converts an internal time value to a readable format, for example 'Mon Sep 25 14:32:27 MET 1995'. It uses the ctime package that comes with Perl.

---

[1] ftp://ftp.informatik.rwth-aachen.de/pub/packages/procmail/

```
1   # Convert current date/time to a neat string.
2   sub timetostr {
3       local ($result);
4
5       require 'ctime.pl';
6       chop($result = &ctime(time));
7
8       # Return result.
9       $result;
10  }
```

The subroutine `timetolog` converts an internal time value into six strings, for example '04', 'Apr', '1995', '09', '23' and '20'. These can be used for printing, or to form patterns for log file analysis.

```
1   # timetolog - convert time to six strings as used in Web server
2   # logfiles, e.g. 04 Apr 1995 09 23 20
3   #
4   sub timetolog {
5       local ($time) = @_;
6       local ($sec, $min, $hour, $mday, $mon, $year,
7              $wday, @dontcare) = localtime ($time);
8       local ($month) = ('Jan','Feb','Mar','Apr','May','Jun',
9                         'Jul','Aug','Sep','Oct','Nov','Dec')[$mon];
10      # localtime returns years as two digits only... guess.
11      $year = ($year>=70) ? $year+1900 : $year+2000;
12      # Turn it into a string.
13      $year = "$year";
14      # Same for $mday, add leading zero if needed.
15      $mday = ($mday < 10) ? "0$mday" : "$mday";
16      # And for $hour, $min, $sec.
17      $hour = ($hour < 10) ? "0$hour" : "$hour";
18      $min = ($min < 10)   ? "0$min" : "$min";
19      $sec = ($sec < 10)   ? "0$sec" : "$sec";
20      # Return result as a tuple.
21      ($mday, $month, $year, $hour, $min, $sec);
22  }
```

5.2.6   Sending electronic mail

Gateway programs frequently need to send electronic mail messages, for example to confirm requests, or to send notification messages to systems administrators. Gateway programs can also use electronic mail to signal error situations. Since they run as independent processes, gateway programs have few other means of attracting the user's attention.

Unfortunately the method of sending electronic mail is very operating system dependent. The following subroutine works only in a Unix environment since it uses the Unix program *sendmail*.

```
1   # sendmail is a convenient routine to send e-mail from a program.
2   # It requires the sendmail program to be in a standard location.
3   #
4   # Typical use:
5   #
6   #    $user = "webmaster@master.web";
7   #    $subj = "Message from the Web";
8   #    $message = "...text with embedded newlines...";
9   #    &sendmail ($user, $subj, $message);
10
11  sub sendmail {
12      local ($to, $subj, $message) = @_;
```

```
13      local ($sendmail) = "/usr/lib/sendmail";
14
15      open (MAIL, "|$sendmail -t > /dev/null 2>&1") ||
16          die ("Error opening pipe to $sendmail: $!\n");
17
18      print MAIL ("To: ", $to, "\n",
19                  "Subject: ", $subj, "\n\n",
20                  $message);
21
22      close (MAIL) ||
23          die ("Error closing pipe to $sendmail: $!\n");
24  }
```

The routine opens a pipe to the *sendmail* program and writes the information through the pipe. Although both the open and close calls are checked for success, errors concerning pipes tend to show up only in the close operation. The path name of the sendmail program, as set at line 13, is appropriate for most Unix systems. Alternative locations are /etc/sendmail and /usr/sbin/sendmail.

The sendmail program is invoked using the '-t' command line option, which makes the program take all its necessary data (such as the recipient, the message subject, and also the message text itself) from its standard input, hence the print statement at lines 18–20 first outputs the recipient and subject information, followed by a blank line, before outputting the text of the message.

Changing the sender address

Under some circumstances, you may wish to change the sender address (the 'From:' field) of the automatic message, for example when a confirmation message is sent out after an electronic registration. It is undesirable to have users sending replies to the Web server's user ID. It may be preferable for such mail messages to come from a local mail name like 'office@mysite.domain'. This can be achieved by using the '-f' flag of sendmail, altering line 13 to:

```
local($sendmail) = "/usr/lib/sendmail -f office\@mysite.domain";
```

Please note that this flag can only be used by so called *trusted* users (normally root, daemon, and uucp). It may be necessary to change the sendmail configuration in order to make this flag work for a gateway script. The corresponding lines in the sendmail configuration file (usually /etc/sendmail.cf or /usr/lib/sendmail.cf) look like this:

```
###   Trusted users
T root daemon uucp
```

For details on *sendmail* see [Hunt92] or [Cost93].

5.3 Processing CGI input

When a gateway program is executed by the server, the request data can be passed in three ways: as command line arguments, in environment variable

QUERY_STRING or in the standard input stream. Since environment variable QUERY_STRING is set even in the case of command line arguments, the program needs to deal with only two cases: QUERY_STRING for GET requests and standard input for POST requests. The routine cgiparse, defined in Section 5.2.2, handles both cases.

5.3.1   Handling data from an ISINDEX request

After calling the routine cgiparse to fetch the data, the associative array returned contains the keywords.

```
%request = &cgiparse();
foreach $keyword ( sort(keys(%request)) ) {
    ... handle $keyword ...
}
```

Depending on the application, sorting the keys may be optional.

5.3.2   Handling data from an ISMAP request

When the user clicks on an image that has the ISMAP attribute set, the pixel coordinates of the click are sent to the gateway program, separated from each other by a comma. By convention, the lower-left pixel (origin) of the image has coordinates 1, 1. As usual, the first number denotes the number of pixels right of the origin, and the second number the number of pixels above the origin, thus the upper-right corner of an image of sixteen pixels high and forty pixels wide would have coordinates 40, 16.

The data is received by the gateway program as a single string which is stored in the associative array. Processing is straighforward:

```
%request = &cgiparse();
($x,$y) = split(',',(keys(%request))[0]);
... process $x and $y ...
```

If the data received by the gateway program really originated from the ISMAP element of an html document the coordinates are unlikely to contain values that lie outside the dimensions of the image, but nevertheless it is considered good programming practice to verify them. In all cases, the gateway program should *never* fail or produce incorrect results when out-of-range values are received.

5.3.3   Handling data from a FORM request

In this case the associative array contains an element for each name of the name–value pairs received; however, there may be more than one value associated with each name. Every element of the array corresponds to a named input field in the form. It is common practice to process only the elements that are expected and ignore name–value pairs with unknown names.

Usually some field values must fulfill specific criteria and some may be compulsory. The first thing to be done after calling `cgiparse` is to check this. For example:

```
%request = &cgiparse();
unless ( defined $request{'Name'} ) {
    ... error: You didn't fill in your name ...
}
unless ( defined $request{'Age'} ) {
    ... error: You didn't fill in your age ...
}
elsif ( $request{'Age'} !~ /^\d+$/ ) {
    ... error: Invalid value for 'Age' ...
}
```

All information should be verified as far as possible. Information is often stored on the server system for later processing by a separate application program. It is much easier to request the user to correct erroneous data at this stage, than for the application program to process it correctly after a time lapse. Moreover, if the data submitted by the user is accepted by the gateway program, the user will assume the data was correct.

If multiple errors are detected they should all be returned to the client. In Section 5.5 a method for doing this given.

Most input fields on a form can have VALUE attributes associated (Section 3.5.1). Upon submission this value will be sent to the server if appropriate.

- For most fields, such as simple text or password fields, the value sent is the value in the field when the form is submitted.

- Radio buttons and checkboxes send their value attributes only if they are checked, although they too can have default values.

- SELECT fields send the value attributes of the currently selected options. If more than one option is selected the values are sent as separate name–value pairs. The routine `cgiparse` detects this and concatenates the values (Section 5.2.2).

5.4   Testing and debugging

The major complicating factor when developing a gateway program is that the program is normally invoked by the Web server. There is no control over when the program will be run, and it could be invoked several times simultaneously, possibly causing concurrency problems. Also, it runs in a minimal environment, explicitly set up by the server. On a Unix system, the following constraints are most likely to cause unexpected problems.

Finding Perl and the Perl library files

The location of Perl is indicated by the first line of the Perl program:

```
#!/usr/local/bin/perl
```

This works on most modern Unix systems, which look at the first line of an executable script, and if it starts with the string '#!' assume that what follows is the name of the interpreter for the script. If your system does not support this technique, you can start the script with the following lines:

```
#!/usr/local/bin/perl
eval exec /usr/local/bin/perl -S $0 $*
    if $running_under_some_shell;
```

Should the system ignore the first line and feed the program to the standard shell (/bin/sh), the latter will start to execute the program as a shell script. The second line given here is valid both as a Perl statement (modified by the line following) and as a shell command, which starts up the Perl interpreter to execute the script. The variables $0 and $* contain the name of the script being executed and the arguments to the script respectively. On some systems $0 doesn't always contain the full path name of the program, so the option '-S' is specified to tell Perl to search for the program if necessary. When Perl locates the program, it parses the lines and ignores the second line because it is continued and made conditional by the third line – the variable $running_under_some_shell will not be true so the condition fails.

If the Perl gateway program requires files from custom Perl libraries these locations must be registered in the program. The standard location for the Perl library is usually compiled into the Perl program itself. Within a Perl program the locations that are searched for library files are registered in the array @INC. The following command runs Perl to show the compiled-in value for @INC:

```
perl -e 'print "@INC\n"'
```

This will return information such as:

```
/usr/local/bin/perl5 .
```

Note the trailing dot, which indicates the current directory. Custom locations can be added as follows:

```
push(@INC, "/usr/custom/perl");      # append
unshift(@INC, "/usr/custom/perl");   # prepend
```

Finding external programs

The search path for external programs, as set by the environment variable PATH, usually contains only a few standard locations. If the gateway program depends on external programs it is best to set the environment variable PATH explicitly to make sure that these programs can be found. A good candidate to add to PATH is the system's directory for local programs, usually /usr/local/bin. Alternatively, programs can be designated by full path name instead of a program name that needs the searching of PATH.

Handling run-time errors

When a Web server runs a gateway program, it expects the program to produce a new document on its standard output stream, STDOUT. Since error messages and diagnostics are usually written to the standard error stream, STDERR, these will not be detected and will disappear without being seen. A call to the Perl routine die (or any other fatal error) will cause the program to terminate silently – any error message will be discarded. This can be avoided by connecting STDERR to STDOUT and using eval to trap otherwise fatal errors:

```
close(STDERR);
open(STDERR,'>&STDOUT');
print STDOUT ('Content-Type: text/html', "\n");
eval { &main; };
print STDOUT ('A fatal error occured: ', $@, "\n") if $@;
subroutine main {
    ... this contains the real code to do the job ...
}
```

Although a file already open on a file variable is implicitly closed when the file variable is used in an open statement, STDERR should be closed explicitly since this file is usually unbuffered. Merely re-opening it would cause an unexpected mix of STDERR and STDOUT output. The Content-Type header is written out as early as possible so any output of the program will be passed by the server to the browser program.

The real work has all been put in a single subroutine, called main, which is called within an eval statement to trap calls to die and other fatal errors. Should an error occur then the associated error message will be placed in the special variable $@. Note the peculiar syntax of Perl requires a semicolon *after* the closing brace of the eval.

Accessing the local file system

When the gateway program is run by the server it normally runs under a user ID that, for security reasons, allows only very limited access to the local file system. This can be a real problem if the program must consult, or worse still, update local files. The difficulty might be overcome by making the local files accessible by everyone on the system. Depending on your system configuration, this may be an option. A better solution would be to run the program under a user ID that allows for the desired access. This user ID might be specifically created for this purpose. To grant access rights to a program it can be made *setuid* (set user ID) or *setgid* (set group ID). A setuid program runs with the access rights of the owner of the program, the *effective user ID*, instead of the user who runs it, the *real user ID*. When it is setgid the same applies for the group IDs. Unfortunately, on most systems it is a well-known security risk to give setuid facilities to an interpreted script and Perl, being aware of this, refuses to run setuid programs on these systems. Therefore a small *wrapper* program, typically written in C as in the following example, must be used to exploit the setuid facility in a safe way before transferring control to the Perl program.

```
 1  #include <stdio.h>
 2
 3  main (argc, argv)
 4  int argc;
 5  char *argv[];
 6  {
 7    char *prog = "/usr/local/lib/webmaster/cgi-script";
 8    argv[0] = "cgi-script";
 9
10    /* Change identity */
11    if (setgid(getegid()) < 0) exit(88);
12    if (setuid(geteuid()) < 0) exit(89);
13
14    /* Execute the Perl program */
15    return execv (prog, argv);
16  }
```

At line 7 the name of the real gateway program is specified. The program sets its user and group IDs to the desired values (lines 11–12) and then executes the Perl program (line 15). Note that it is mandatory to set both the user and group IDs, otherwise Perl will refuse to execute the program, and also that the group ID should be set before the user ID, since changing the user ID could cause the loss of the privilege to change group ID.

This wrapper program should be compiled and installed with the appropriate user and group ownership, and setuid and setgid permissions, in a location where the Web server expects gateway programs to reside (the *exec path*, Section 4).

5.4.1   Stand-alone testing

To return the desired results, the gateway program must perform the following tasks:

- Pick up the data sent to it by the client via the server.

- Decode the data into the proper format.

- Check the data for consistency.

- Process the data, possibly involving other data stored in local files, and generate results.

- Send the results back to the server in HTML format.

All except the first task can be tested and verified offline by running the program manually. Of course, the program must be syntactically correct, and the constraints described above should be kept in mind during program development.

When testing the program we strongly advise invoking Perl with the '-w' command line option, which instructs Perl to perform extensive additional checking on the program. For example, it will notify the use of undefined variables, potential typographical errors and much more. Use version 5 of Perl if possible, as it incorporates some useful enhancements in this area. Warnings should be eliminated as early as possible during program development. This way the appearance of new warnings is very likely to signal programming errors or possible unexpected behavior.

In general, most warnings can be avoided by introducing every variable (with a local or my statement) and assigning it an appropriate initial value.

For testing purposes it is often convenient to supply data to the gateway program via command line arguments or standard input. The following piece of code implements this:

```
 1   # If this script is called manually, run in test mode.
 2   unless ( defined $ENV{'SCRIPT_NAME'} ) {
 3       print STDOUT ("$0 was not invoked from the server!\n");
 4       if ( @ARGV > 0 ) {
 5           print STDOUT ("Using command line arguments.\n");
 6           $request = join('&', @ARGV);
 7       }
 8       else {
 9           print STDOUT ("Please enter the name/value pairs ",
10                        "URL-encoded on the standard input.\n");
11           while ( <> ) {
12               # Trim trailing newline.
13               chop;
14               # Add it using & separator.
15               $request .= $_ . '&';
16           }
17           # Chop trailing '&'.
18           chop ($request);
19       }
20   }
21   # Parse it.
22   %request = &cgiparse($request);
```

This example demonstrates why we have equipped the subroutine cgiparse with an optional parameter. When a program containing this code is run manually, it will allow name–value pairs to be entered on the standard input. Data can be typed in directly, or read from a file using redirection of standard input. The input must be URL-encoded. The automatic encoding of test data can easily be added, and is left as an exercise for the reader.

On the last line of the example, the routine cgiparse is called with the contents of $request. When the program is invoked by the server, the environment variable SCRIPT_NAME will be defined hence, there will be no input done here. $request will be left undefined which causes cgiparse to collect the data as described in Section 5.2.2.

The rest of the program can use the condition 'defined $request', for example to conditionally output debugging information, which can speed up the development of gateway programs tremendously. However, care must be taken to avoid writing debugging code that introduces unwanted side effects, for example:

```
if ( defined $request ) {
    print STDERR ("Now processing record ", ++$recnr, "\n")
}
```

Variable $recnr will *only* be incremented if the program is run manually, which is very likely to cause unexpected results when the program is run by the Web server.

For more extensive debugging the Perl interactive debugger can be used. This allows the interrogation and modification of program variables, the setting of breakpoints in the program, and single-stepping through the program. The debugger is started by invoking Perl with the '-d' command line option.

To avoid corrupting live data during testing, any database names in the program should be modified to point to test databases. Similarly, change email addresses to your private email address so you can easily track messages. However make sure that changing the configuration values does not inadvertently introduce bugs.

Once manual testing shows that the program appears to function correctly, the output from the program, which must be a valid HTML document, should be inspected using a Web browser. The output can be redirected to a file; however, the initial Content-Type header will have to be removed. By redirecting only the standard output stream, it is possible to detect misdirected output, for example data written to the error stream that should have been written to the output stream instead.

Picking up the request data from the server environment variables can be simulated by manually setting the necessary environment variables before running the program, using the Unix *env* command, for example:

```
env SCRIPT_NAME=cgi-program \
    REQUEST_METHOD=GET QUERY_STRING='name1=val1&name2=%22val2%22' \
    CONTENT_LENGTH=0 \
        perl -w cgi-program.pl
```

Finally, remove the current environment completely by passing an initial '-' argument to *env*, and verify that everything still works:

```
env - SCRIPT_NAME=cgi-program \
    REQUEST_METHOD=GET QUERY_STRING='name1=val1&name2=%22val2%22' \
    CONTENT_LENGTH=0 \
        /usr/local/bin/perl -w cgi-program.pl
```

Note that the full path name for Perl should be supplied in this case, since the total environment will be cleared, including the search path for programs (PATH).

Regression testing

In the examples above it is important that the program returns data (the HTML document) that can be captured in a file. Subsequent runs of the program with identical input data should produce identical output data. This can be verified by capturing the new data and comparing it to the original data. Using this technique, known as *regression testing*, test suites can be built, which automatically verify that modifications to the program did not introduce changes to the expected output. Special software packages are available to support this type of testing, such as the *DejaGNU* package from the Free Software Foundation[2].

5.4.2   Testing under the server

When the gateway program appears to work stand-alone, it should then be tested under a real Web server. If possible, a separate Web server should be set up for this

---

[2]ftp://ftp.prep.ai.mit.edu/pub/gnu/

purpose. The major advantage to be gained is the ease and speed with which log files from a private server can be inspected, compared with those from a production server, which may process and log thousands of requests each hour. If possible, use a dedicated system to run this Web server to prevent the production environment influencing the test environment, and vice versa. It is usually possible to start up a Web server manually without the need for system administration privileges. However, in this case the server will not be able to change its user ID, so gateway programs will be executed using your own ID and associated privileges. It must be borne in mind that this will be different from the actual production environment.

5.4.3   Using the CERN server

The difficulties involved in setting up a private server depend on the server used. Setting up a private version of the CERN 3.0 server is very easy. Assuming that private server documents are stored in the directory /home/me/public_html and that gateway programs reside in /home/me/cgi-bin, a configuration file, config.tst, can be created containing the lines:

```
Exec    /cgi-bin/*      /home/me/cgi-bin/*
Pass    /*              /home/me/public_html/*
```

and the server started manually with

```
httpd -p 8080 -r config.tst -v
```

This will start the server and have it listen on port 8080 (any number above 1024 may be chosen, but some ports may already be in use by other programs). The command line option '-v' causes the server to generate debugging messages, which can be used to track the server's behavior and possible problems.

Now the server can be contacted with a Web browser program specifying the URL http://localhost:8080/. Alternatively, the *telnet* program can be used to communicate directly with the server emulating a browser, as follows:

```
telnet localhost 8080
Trying 127.0.0.1...
Connected to localhost.
Escape character is '^]'.
GET / HTTP/1.0
                <= enter a blank line to terminate the request
...output from the server...
```

Interpreting the debugging messages requires skill. It is necessary to have some knowledge of the server's internal workings to understand their precise meaning, but even without understanding the server internals in detail, the messages provide a good deal of useful information. For example, consider the following debugging messages from a server run (note that a number of lines of less relevant information have been removed from this excerpt):

```
1  ...........  This is CERN-HTTPD, version 3.0, using libwww 2.17
2  Daemon......  accepting connection...
3  TCP........  Peer name is 'localhost'
4  Reading.....  socket 4 from host 127.0.0.1
5  User-Agent..  Mozilla/1.1N (X11; I; SunOS 4.1.3_U1 sun4c)
```

Lines 2–5 indicate a connection being made. The client program is Netscape, which identifies itself as `Mozilla`.

```
 6   HTSimplify.. '/Welcome.html' into
 7   ........... '/Welcome.html'
 8   Pass........ rule matched "/Welcome.html"
 9               -> "/home/me/public_html/Welcome.html"
10   Passing..... "/home/me/public_html/Welcome.html"
11   Content-Length 3264
12   Last-Modified Monday, 03-Jul-95 19:33:18 GMT
```

Lines 6–10 show that the request for a file named `Welcome.html` is mapped to file name of the document on disk by the `Pass` statement in the configuration file. Some of the file's properties are shown.

```
13   Translated.. "/home/me/public_html/Welcome.html"
14   HTAccess.... Loading document /Welcome.html
15   LoadFile.... Looking for '/home/me/public_html/Welcome.html'
16   Local filename is "/home/me/public_html/Welcome.html"
17   HTLoadFile.. Accessing local file system.
18   HTLoadFile.. Opened '/home/me/public_html/Welcome.html'
19               on local file system
```

The document file is then opened.

```
20   ........... Headers for the client
21   HTTP/1.0 200 Document follows
22   MIME-Version: 1.0
23   Server: CERN/3.0
24   Date: Tuesday, 15-Aug-95 10:54:28 GMT
25   Content-Type: text/html
26   Content-Length: 3264
27   Last-Modified: Monday, 03-Jul-95 19:33:18 GMT
28
29   ........... End of headers
```

Lines 20–29 show the response headers that were constructed (note the blank line that terminates the headers).

```
30   Already..... known content-length: 3264
31   HTAccess.... '/Welcome.html' has been accessed.
```

The headers, as shown, and the document itself are then passed to the browser program.

Now consider the case of a form with the following definition:

```
<form action="http://localhost:8080/cgi-bin/echo" method="get">
<input name="foo">
<input name="bar">
<input type=submit>
</form>
```

This will result in the following server debugging messages (again, a number of lines of irrelevant information have been removed).

```
1   ........... This is CERN-HTTPD, version 3.0, using libwww 2.17
2   Daemon...... accepting connection...
3   TCP........ Peer name is 'localhost'
4   Reading..... socket 4 from host 127.0.0.1
5   Referer..... file://localhost/home/me/book/t.html
6   User-Agent.. Mozilla/1.1N (X11; I; SunOS)
```

Lines 2–5 again show a connection being made. Note that the name of the document that originates this request, the referer, is passed to the server.

```
 7  HTSimplify.. '/cgi-bin/echo' into
 8  ........... '/cgi-bin/echo'
 9  Exec....... rule matched "/cgi-bin/echo"
10             -> "/home/me/public_html/cgi-bin/echo"
11  Script call.
12  Resolving... calling scheme for "/home/me/public_html/cgi-bin/echo"
13  Found out... no .pp suffix, directly executable
```

In line 9 the server determines that a gateway program is to be called as the `Exec` statement in the configuration file is matched.

```
14  Scheme...... CGI/1.1
15  Environ..... SERVER_SOFTWARE=CERN/3.0
16  Environ..... SERVER_NAME=squirrel.nl.net
17  Environ..... SERVER_PORT=8080
18  Environ..... GATEWAY_INTERFACE=CGI/1.1
19  Environ..... SERVER_PROTOCOL=HTTP/1.0
20  Environ..... REQUEST_METHOD=GET
21  Environ..... PATH_INFO=
22  Environ..... PATH_TRANSLATED=
23  Environ..... QUERY_STRING=foo=xaxa&bar=
24  Environ..... SCRIPT_NAME=/cgi-bin/echo
25  Environ..... REMOTE_HOST=localhost
26  Environ..... REMOTE_ADDR=127.0.0.1
27  Environ..... AUTH_TYPE=
28  Environ..... REMOTE_USER=
29  Environ..... REMOTE_IDENT=
30  Environ..... REFERER_URL=file://localhost/home/me/book/t.html
31  Environ..... HTTP_ACCEPT=*/*, image/gif, image/jpeg
32  Environ..... HTTP_USER_AGENT=Mozilla/1.1N (X11; I; SunOS)
33  Environ..... HTTP_REFERER=file://localhost/home/me/book/t.html
```

The environment, as defined in the CGI specification, is constructed.

```
34  Info....... HTScriptArgv: returning:
35  argv[0] = "echo"
36  TimeOut..... set for process 24389 (300 secs)
37  Child....... is alive
38  Child...... doing IO redirections
39  Child...... stdout to pipe
40  Child...... done
41  Child...... Standalone specific IO redirections done.
42  Child...... redirecting stderr to stdout, and then doing execve()
```

The gateway program is invoked.

```
43  Ok......... script result content-type text/html
44  Calculating. content-length on the fly
45
46  Calculated.. content-length: 2686
```

The program executes successfully, and its output is read by the server.

```
47  HTTP header. length: 156 bytes
48  ........... Headers for the client
49  HTTP/1.0 200 Document follows
50  MIME-Version: 1.0
51  Server: CERN/3.0
52  Date: Tuesday, 15-Aug-95 12:02:27 GMT
53  Content-Type: text/html
54  Content-Length: 2686
55
56  ........... End of headers
57  Parent...... child pid 24389 has finished
```

The headers for the client are constructed, and finally, the headers plus the program output are sent to the client.

Before running a new gateway program, run some programs that are known to work, as a means of familiarizing yourself with the server messages.

5.4.4   Interpreting log files

If it is not possible to use a private server, often the only information about what is happening can be found in the server log files. Most servers use a common log file format, which is easy to read (for the human as well as for log file analyzing programs). This format, and how to interpret it, is described in Section 6.2.

5.4.5   Into production

During the testing the gateway program configuration may have been modified, to avoid interacting with the real production environment. Before putting the new program into production, these changes need to be undone. Also, do not forget to remove or disable the debugging code when the program goes into production!

5.5   Dissection of a real example

This section contains a detailed description of a real, working program. In this section we use many of the routines and mechanisms previously discussed.

The following program is a gateway program that, when initially invoked, presents the user with a small form to fill in and submit. The request data is then sent to the same program which checks the data for validity and completeness, and stores it for further processing.

```
1   #!/usr/local/bin/perl
2
3   # wing-form.pl -- simple registration interface.
4   #
```

We assume that the system can handle the #! construct to invoke the Perl interpreter.

```
5    ############### Configuration ###############
6    #
7    # Title or name of your server:
8    #    Example: $title = 'ICE Indexing Gateway';
9    $title ='';
10
11   # The program can send mail, append data to a file, or both.
12   # Who to send mail to:
13   #    Example: $mailto = 'webmaster@master.web';
14   $mailto = '';
15
16   # Where to store the data:
17   #    Example: $outfile = '/usr/spool/webmaster/requests.dat';
18   $outfile = '';
19
20   ############### End of Configuration ###############
```

A descriptive title for the form that will be presented to the user is required and must be assigned to the variable $title in line 9.

The program can store the user data in a local file, in which case variable $out-file needs to be set. Alternatively, the user data can be sent by electronic mail, in which case the variable $mailto must be set. It is also possible to set both variables to exploit both alternatives.

```perl
21   # Send the HTTP header
22   &send_header();
23
24   # Do the real work, trapping run-time errors.
25   eval { &main; };
26
27   # If a run-time error has occured, log it to STDOUT.
28   if ( $@ ) {
29       &html_start("Error in Script");
30       print STDOUT ("$@\n");
31       &html_end();
32       exit(1);
33   }
```

To trap run-time errors, all processing is executed from a subroutine, main, that is called within an eval statement. Run-time errors, including calls to the Perl function die, will cause execution to abort and to resume with the next statement after the eval. The Perl variable $@ is set to contain the reason for the failure. If a run-time error was trapped an error message is included in an HTML document and sent to the user. The main line of code for this program ends here. The remainder of the file contains the necessary subroutines.

```perl
34   ############### Subroutines ###############
35
36   sub main {
37
38       # Check configuration.
39       unless ( $outfile ne '' || $mailto ne '' ) {
40           die("Configuration error: ".
41               "need to set \$mailto and/or \$outfile.\n");
42       }
43       unless ( $title ne '' ) {
44           die("Configuration error: ".
45               "\$title hasn't been set.\n");
46       }
```

As previously stated, subroutine main contains all the work that needs to be done. First, the configuration is checked. Variable $title needs to be set, as does at least one of $mailto and $outfile. Such configuration errors are only likely to occur the very first time the program is run.

```perl
47       # If this script is called manually, run in test mode.
48       unless ( defined $ENV{'SCRIPT_NAME'} ) {
49           print STDOUT ("$0 was not invoked from the server!\n");
50           if ( @ARGV > 0 ) {
51               print STDOUT ("Using command line arguments.\n");
52               $request = join('&', @ARGV);
53           }
54           else {
55               print STDOUT ("Please enter the name/value pairs ",
56                             "URL-encoded on the standard input.\n");
57               while ( <> ) {
58                   # Trim trailing newline.
59                   chop;
```

```
60              # Add it using & separator.
61              $request .= $_ . '&';
62          }
63          # Chop trailing '&'.
64          chop($request);
65      }
66  }
```

Next the request data is collected. This program supports all possible sources of data: the GET and POST requests, and test input via command line arguments or standard input. The code fragment above handles the case of test input. Other methods are handled by the routine cgiparse that will be called later on.

```
67      # Do we have input?
68      if ( (!defined $request) &&
69          $ENV{'CONTENT_LENGTH'} == 0 &&
70          $ENV{'QUERY_STRING'} eq '' ) {
71
72          # No input. Send the form.
73          &html_start($title);
74          &send_form();
75          &html_end();
76          return;
77      }
```

Here a check is made for the presence of input. If there is no input, this gateway program apparently is not invoked as the result of submitting a form. In this case there are two alternatives. One alternative is to send the form itself back to the user, the approach chosen here. The other possibility is to complain, which, of course, is only reasonable if the form resides elsewhere.

```
78      # Parse forms result and store it in an associative array.
79      %forms = &cgiparse($request);
```

The routine cgiparse is called to fetch the request data from GET or POST requests, and to parse it into the associative array %forms. The variable $request is passed to cgiparse if test data was input earlier.

```
80      # Check the user data.
81      # We check everything we can, and issue multiple error
82      # messages if needed.
83      local ($err) = 0;
84      local ($msg) = '';
85      unless ( (defined $forms{'LaNa'}) && $forms{'LaNa'} ne '' ) {
86          $err++;
87          $msg .= "<LI>Your last name was not filled in.\n";
88      }
89      unless ( (defined $forms{'FiNa'}) && $forms{'FiNa'} ne '' ) {
90          $err++;
91          $msg .= "<LI>Your first name was not filled in\n";
92      }
93      unless ( (defined $forms{'CoNa'}) && $forms{'CoNa'} ne '' ) {
94          $err++;
95          $msg .= "<LI>Your company name was not filled in\n";
96      }
97      if ( $err ) {
98          &html_start("Error processing user data");
99          print STDOUT ("<UL>\n", $msg, "</UL>\n");
100         print STDOUT ("<P>Please fill in de necessary data ",
101                       "and submit again.\n");
102         &html_end();
103         return;
104     }
```

There are three fields which must be filled in by the user. In the above code fragment all three are checked. For every field not filled in we append an error message in the form of an HTML list element to the variable $msg and increment the error counter $err.

By checking $err it is possible to determine if there were any data errors, in which case a complete HTML document is created, containing the error messages accumulated above, and passed to the user.

```
105     # Construct the message string. Expect problems here
106     # if the CGI data contains strange characters...
107     local ($querytext) = '';
108     foreach $w ( sort(keys(%forms)) ) {
109         $querytext .= "$w = $forms{$w}\n";
110     }
```

Here we construct a string $querytext that contains the request data in a more friendly format, for example.

```
FiNa = John
LaNa = Doe
...
```

As pointed out in the program comments, if the user data contains strange characters, such as embedded newlines, this can cause misleading results. Care must be taken when interpreting the data.

```
111     &html_start($title);
```

Now we have checked and verified everything, so we can prepare the confirmation document.

```
112     # Send mail, if requested.
113     if ( $mailto ne '' ) {
114         &sendmail($mailto, 'Request from the Web', $querytext);
115     }
```

Using the routine sendmail, the request data is sent by electronic mail to the designated email address.

```
116     # Append the info to the data file, if requested.
117     if ( $outfile ne '' ) {
118         if ( open(FP, "+>>$outfile") ) {
119             local ($timstr) = &timetostr();
120             &lockfile(FP);          # lock exclusive
121             seek(FP, 0, 2);         # position at end
122             # Append the data.
123             print FP ("-------------------\n",
124                       "Date: ", $timstr, "\n",
125                       $querytext, "\n");
126             close(FP);
127         }
128         else {
129             print STDOUT ("<p>Error: ",
130                           "The database could not be updated.\n",
131                           "Please report this error to\n",
132                           "\"$mailto\"\n",
133                           "together with the following ",
134                           "information:<BR>\n",
135                           "<PRE>$querytext<PRE>\n");
136             &html_end();
137             return;
138         }
139     }
```

This code fragment handles the case where the request data must be stored on the local file system. The subroutine `lockfile` is used to prevent problems with concurrent access. The information added to the file will look like:

```
- - - - - - - - - - - - - - - - - - -
Date: Fri Aug 11 18:58:42 1995
FiNa = John
LaNa = Doe
...
```

It is assumed that some other program will eventually process the contents of this file.

```
140        # Notify the user.
141        print STDOUT ("<p>Thank you for registering.\n",
142                      "<p>This was your data:<BR>");
143        print STDOUT ("<PRE>$querytext<PRE>\n");
```

If all goes well, let the user know that the request was processed.

```
144        # Finish.
145        &html_end();
146    }
```

This ends the subroutine `main`.

```
147    sub send_form {
148        local ($scriptname) = $ENV{'SCRIPT_NAME'};
149
150        print STDOUT ("<FORM ACTION=\"$scriptname\" ",
151                      "METHOD=\"POST\">\n");
```

The subroutine `send_form` constructs the form and adds it to the standard output. The environment variable `SCRIPT_NAME` is used to get the actual URL for the gateway program so it can be used in the `ACTION` attribute of the `<FORM>`. This example uses the `POST` method, but the `GET` method would work equally well.

```
152        print STDOUT <<'ENDHTML';
153        <HR>
154        <H3>How you access Stepwise</H3>
155        Please select the appropriate value:<BR>
156
157        Type of machine:
158        <SELECT NAME="TyMa">
159        <OPTION> Nextstep for Intel
160        <OPTION> NeXT
161        <OPTION> Mac
162        <OPTION> PC
163        <OPTION> other
164        </SELECT>
165        <P>
166        <HR>
167
168        <H3>Information on your person</H3>
169        Please fill in the following fields,
170        and then hit the "Ok" button
171        to transfer the values to our database:
172        <P><B>
173        First name    <BR>  <INPUT NAME="FiNa"  SIZE=40><P>
174        Last name     <BR>  <INPUT NAME="LaNa"  SIZE=40><P>
175        Company name  <BR>  <INPUT NAME="CoNa"  SIZE=40><P>
176        </B>
177
178        <HR>
179    ENDHTML
180
```

```
181      print STDOUT ("<P>Transfer the values and send them via\n",
182                    "email to \"$mailto\":<P>\n",
183                    "<INPUT TYPE=\"submit\" VALUE=\" Ok \">\n",
184                    "<HR>\n");
185
186  }
```

The form consists of a selection field, three input fields and a submit button.

Final remarks

There are several ways to increase the user friendliness of forms interfaces. For example, when the user receives an error message, he or she must manually return to the form using the browser's Back button. It is possible to include a new instance of the form with the error message, and use the data already present to provide initial values for the fields on the forms. An example of this technique can be found in Section A.6.

Another enhancement might be to make submission a staged process. This could be done by generating a new form, showing all the data the user has entered, with a confirmation button to accept these values, and a cancel button, to go back and re-edit the data.

At the data level, application dependent semantic consistency checks should be performed, as extensively as possible. Numbers, such as a person's age, ISBN numbers and so on, can be verified. The end result will be user data that is easy to process further.

6

Enhancing Server Functionality

The previous chapters have dealt with the underlying standards and protocols of Web server technology, and introduced the Common Gateway Interface for including the output of external programs into a server's document space. We will now show some examples of how gateway programs can be used to augment servers with additional functionality, such as searching and the automatic creation of connectivity reports and usage charts. We will also show how gateway programs can be created to access information that is stored in different formats, or resides in other data repositories. Gateways serve as Web compatible interfaces to otherwise inaccessible services, and make information available to Web browsers without the necessity of replicating it. We will cover both dynamic and static gateways. The former generate information through a dynamic process, while the latter act as format converters that translate one data representation into another.

6.1   Searchable repositories

One of the biggest problems with the World Wide Web is locating relevant information. This is partly caused by the fact that current server technology offers no built-in search facility. In fact, servers do not know anything about the documents they serve until those documents are actually requested.

Search functionality can be provided as an add-on through gateway programs. Not only can a gateway program be used to provide free text searches (for example via an interface to a WAIS server or a full text database), but by using special HTML elements to add information *about* the document (meta-information), keyword and topic based searches can also be provided. By including other file attributes such as the size or the date of last modification, a searchable repository can provide users with a variety of search options. A draw-back of this method is that all HTML documents must be provided with meta-information. Depending on the way the documents are produced this can be a time-consuming and costly process.

Examples of possible search options include:

- Documents by a specific author, or in a specific language.

- Files that were modified in the last few days.

- Articles containing a given keyword.

- All documents containing the word 'Scoobee-Doo' in their title.

Of course, meta-information can also be used to map any internal classification or naming scheme such as ISBN to hypertext documents. In this section, we show how document meta-information can be incorporated into documents, and how it can be extracted and stored in global index files. By using fill-out forms as front-ends and gateway programs to handle user input, an easy to use interface for retrieving documents can be provided.

6.1.1   Indexing meta-information

Although full text searches of a Web archive are an important way of identifying relevant information, sometimes it can be very useful to base searches on document attributes such as author, keywords, language, etc. The HTML specification defines a special markup element for this purpose: the meta tag, <META>. This tag can be used to augment documents with information that is not normally displayed by browsers. In addition, HTTP servers can read the content of the document heading to generate response headers corresponding to any element by defining a value for the attribute HTTP-EQUIV. This provides document authors with a mechanism for identifying information that should be included in the response headers for an HTTP request. The markup is stored as attributes of a tag and is not displayed if the document is loaded into a browser. It can however be extracted by servers and clients for use in identifying, indexing, and cataloging documents.

In this section, we show how information stored in the meta tag can be parsed and stored in a simple index file. By providing a gateway to access this index, a Web server can be augmented with a meta-information search facility. It goes without saying that indexing of meta-information can only take place if your documents actually contain meta-information. Unfortunately most HTML preparation tools do not support meta-information yet. For documents without meta-information, full-text search methods are described in the next section.

Here is an example of meta markup. There is no restriction on the number of meta tags per document. In our example, the document header contains two instances of the meta tag, the first defining an attribute 'keywords' with the value 'cdrom' and 'library', the second defining an attribute 'cost' with the value '0.25'.

```
<HEAD>
<TITLE>Electronic Libraries</TITLE>
<META
  name="keywords"
  content="cdrom,library">
<META
  name="cost"
```

```
        content="0.25">
      </HEAD>
      <BODY>
      ...
```

In order to create a searchable index, the meta-information must be extracted and stored in a searchable database. Let's see how such a program can be written.

Traversing a file tree is quite easy using the find package which is part of the Perl distribution. The find routine works as follows. A list of directories to be searched is passed to find. For every file found in the file tree, find sets variables containing the directory path and name of that file, and calls the wanted subroutine, which must be defined.

It is good practice to keep the routine wanted short, if possible, for example by storing the file names in an array, which can be evaluated later. However, for large numbers of documents it is better not to store the file names in an array, but to call indexfile directly from wanted. In this case, wanted should take precautions not to modify the variables used by the find package, especially $_.

```
1   #!/usr/local/bin/perl
2
3   # Create a <META> tag index file.
4
5   # The physical directory/directories to scan for html-files
6   @SEARCHDIRS = ("/Users/neuss/.htmlpub");
7
8   # Location of the index file
9   $INDEXFILE = "/tmp/meta.idx";
10
11  require "find.pl";
12  local (@allfiles);
13
14  open (INDEX, ">$INDEXFILE");
15  &find (@SEARCHDIRS);   # stores file names in @allfiles
16
17  foreach $name ( @allfiles ) {
18      print STDERR ("indexing [$name]\n");
19      &indexfile ($name);
20  }
21
22  # Subroutine 'wanted' will be called by &find().
23  sub wanted {
24      if ( /.html$/ ) {
25          push (@allfiles, $name);
26      }
27  }
```

Next, a subroutine is needed to perform the actual extraction and indexing of tags. First the input file is converted to a form where every tag appears on a single line by itself. This can be achieved by using the '>' character as the input delimiter, putting newlines before and after every tag, and discarding all other newline characters. After this procedure, the input will look like this:

```
<HEAD>
<TITLE>
Electronic Libraries
</TITLE>
<META NAME="keywords" content="cdrom,library">
<META NAME="cost" content="0.25">
</HEAD>
<BODY>
```

The rest is straightforward: since every tag appears on a single line, it can easily be matched with a regular expression and stored in a Perl variable. In order to be able to handle multiple meta tags per document, the attribute–value pairs found are stored in an array.

```
28   # Parse file for META tags and store them in index.
29   sub indexfile {
30       local ($file) = @_;
31       local ($title, $intitle, $metaname, $metacont, @metalist);
32       unless (-r $file && open(FPIN, "$file") ) {
33           # File readable?
34           print STDERR ("$file: $!\n");
35           return;
36       }
37       local ($dev, $ino, $mode, $nlink, $uid, $gid, $rdev, $size,
38              $atime, $mtime, @dontcare) = stat ($file);
39
40       # Set input separator to the tag close character ">".
41       $/ = ">";
42
43       while ( <FPIN> ) {
44           s/\s+/ /g;              # fold whitespaces into a single blank
45           s/([^\n])</\1\n</g; # insert a CR before every '<'..
46           s/>([^\n])/>\n\1/g; # .. and after every '>'
47           foreach ( split (/\n/, $_) ) {
48               # Opening title tag.
49               if ( m:<title>:i ) {
50                   $intitle = "y";
51                   $title = "";
52                   next;
53               }
54               # Closing title tag.
55               if ( m:</title>:i ) {
56                   $intitle = "";
57                   next;
58               }
59               # Meta element.
60               if( m:<meta name=\"(\S+)\"\s+content=\"([^\"]+)\">:i ) {
61                   $metaname = $1;
62                   $metacont = $2;
63                   push (@metalist, "$metaname=$metacont");
64                   next;
65               }
66               # Title string.
67               if ( $intitle && !/</ ) {
68                   $title .= $_;
69               }
70           }
71       }
72       # If any meta tags were found...
73       if ( @metalist > 0 ) {
74           $file =~ tr/\n/ /s;
75           $title =~ tr/\n/ /s;
76           print INDEX ("\@f $file\n");
77           print INDEX ("\@t $title\n");
78           print INDEX ("\@m $mtime\n");
79           foreach $w ( @metalist ) {
80               print INDEX ("$w\n");
81           }
82       }
83       @metalist = "";
84       close (FPIN);
85   }
```

This program generates a simple output format, consisting of the path, document title, and time of last modification, followed by meta-information encoded as attribute–value pairs. By prefixing path, title and modification time with a constant string, they can easily be matched by a routine which searches the meta index for specific keywords. Figure 6.1 shows an excerpt from the meta index file.

```
...
@f /Users/www/docs/Libraries.html
@t Electronic Libraries
@m 784481117
keywords=cdrom,library
cost=0.25
...
```

Figure 6.1   Meta-information index file format

The following code fragment searches an index file in this format, and converts the matches to hyperlinks.

```
1   # Get index entries matching query.
2   sub getmeta {
3       local ($attrib, $value) = @_;
4       local (%list, $grepexpr, $entry, $result);
5       $grepexpr = "$attrib=.*$value.*";
6
7       local ($timstr);
8       open (FPIN, "<$indexfile") || die ("$indexfile: $!\n");
9       while ( <FPIN> ) {
10          next unless /^\@|$grepexpr/i;
11          if ( /^\@/ ) {
12              if ( /\@f\s(.*)$/ ) { $path   = $1; next; }
13              if ( /\@t\s(.*)$/ ) { $title  = $1; next; }
14              if ( /\@m\s(.*)$/ ) { $mtime  = $1; next; }
15          }
16          else {
17              local ($lastmod) = &timetostr ($mtime);
18              unless ($title) {
19                  $title = "(NO TITLE)";
20              }
21              $entry = "<LI><A HREF=\"$path\">".
22                  "<I>$title</I></A><BR>\n";
23              $entry .= "$file (last change: $lastmod)<BR>\n";
24              $list{$path} = $entry;
25          }
26      }
27      close (FPIN);
28
29      # Get the keys that were found.
30      local (@keys) = sort(keys(%list));
31      if ( @keys > 0 ) {
32          $result .= "<UL>\n";
33          foreach $key ( @keys ) {
34              $result .= $list{$key};
35          }
36          $result .= "</UL>\n";
37      }
38      else {
39          $result .= "(no match)\n";
40      }
41      $result;
42  }
```

For the sake of brevity, the code necessary for wrapping this function into a CGI compliant program has been omitted. Code that maps between virtual URL paths and physical file system paths must also be added. A complete listing for a meta-information indexing routine can be found in Section A.4.2.

6.1.2 Performing full-text queries

Providing a full-text search facility goes one step further: it lets users search not only those text parts that are explicitly tagged as 'keywords', but instead identify all those files that contain a given word anywhere in the document body. Various tools and packages that provide full text retrieval for Web servers already exist. One possible approach is to install a WAIS (Wide-Area Information System) server and connect it to the Web with a gateway program. Instructions on installing a WAIS index and connecting it to an CGI compliant Web server can be found on NCSA's server documentation site[1].

Another very powerful system, albeit one that is rather difficult to install, is Harvest[2]. Harvest comprises a set of tools to gather, extract, organize, search, and replicate information across the Internet. Not only does it provide a server local search facility, it also distributes the index and searching across several servers. Harvest requires that the documents conform strictly to the HTML specifications, and since most HTML documents do not fit its criteria its usefulness is rather limited. For a small Web server, installing Harvest might be deemed excessive unless it is intended to make resource discovery information available to the outside world.

In the latter case, the GlimpseHTTP tools[3] may provide a more appropriate solution. They provide a fast and efficient search facility based on the *glimpse* search engine. This search engine, which is also used by Harvest, supports approximate matching (finding misspelled words), Boolean queries, and limited forms of regular expressions.

It is of course also possible to provide a free text search utility following the same approach we used for indexing meta-information in the previous section. The basic approach is to dispose of all HTML tags, store words and their frequency in an associative array, and write the information to an index file. Of course, since this uses a very simple and straightforward index format, such a search tool will not be as fast as the more specialized tools like Harvest or WAIS, but could be perfectly appropriate for a small Web site. Moreover it may even be the only option available for free if your Web server runs on a Macintosh or a Windows NT machine.

The previous section demonstrated how a file index can be created and accessed. We will now consider how an HTML file can be parsed and converted to a list of words for a full-text search.

---

[1] http://hoohoo.ncsa.uiuc.edu/docs/tutorials/wais.html
[2] http://harvest.cs.colorado.edu/harvest/
[3] http://glimpse.cs.arizona.edu:1994/ghttp/

First, an example of an HTML file:

```
<HTML>
<META
  name="keywords"
  content="Web,history,NeXT">
<HEAD><TITLE>History of the Web</TITLE></HEAD>
<BODY>
<!-- provide pointer to Tim's home page -->
<H1 align=center>History of the Web</H1>
Did you know that the first <I>Web browser</I> was written
only six years ago by Tim
Berners-Lee, then with <A href="http://www.cern.ch/">CERN</A>?
And that it was created on a <A href="http://www.next.com/">NeXT</A>
computer?
</BODY>
```

In order to separate the text into single words and tags, the '>' character is used as an input delimiter. Since an HTML tag may never contain an un-encoded '>', every input read will return a complete tag. In addition, every whitespace character is converted to a blank, and a newline inserted before the opening '<'. The following Perl code fragment performs this conversion:

```
1  # Set input separator to the tag close character ">".
2  $/ = ">";
3  while ( <> ) {
4      s/\s+/ /g;                # fold whitespaces into single blank
5      s/(\S+)\s*</\1\n</g;      # insert newline before every '<'
6      print ("$_\n");
7  }
```

After processing by this simple filter, the HTML file looks like this:

```
<HTML>
 <META name="keywords" content="Web,history,NeXT">
 <HEAD>
<TITLE>
History of the Web
</TITLE>
</HEAD>
 <BODY>
 <!-- provide pointer to Tim's home page -->
 <H1 align=center>
History of the Web
</H1>
 Did you know that the first
<I>
Web browser
</I>
 was written only six years ago by Tim Berners-Lee, then with
<A href="http://www.cern.ch/">
CERN
</A>
? And that it was created on a
<A href="http://www.next.com/">
NeXT
</A>
 computer?
</BODY>
```

Since this input has been converted to a sequence of tags interspersed with lines that consist only of text, it is easy to match the tags. This permits the extraction of items such as title or headings. The Perl split function is used to separate input at newline characters, and foreach to iterate over the result:

```
1   #!/usr/local/bin/perl
2
3   # Set input separator to the tag close character ">".
4   $/ = ">";
5
6   while ( <> ) {
7       s/\s+/ /g;                  # fold whitespaces into single blank
8       s/(\S+)\s*</\1\n</g;        # insert newline before every '<'
9       foreach ( split (/\n/ ,$_) ) {
10          # Opening title tag.
11          if ( m:<title>:i ) {
12              $intitle = "y";
13              $title = "";
14          }
15          # Closing title tag.
16          if ( m:</title>:i ) {
17              $intitle = "";
18          }
```

If an input line does not contain a '<' character, it is a text line, in which case it must be parsed into single words and indexed. Testing the flag intitle allows a distinction to be made between text in the title and text in the body of the document. Using the tr function, unwanted characters such as hyphens and punctuation are removed.

```
19          if ( !/</ ) {
20              # Input is not a tag => index word.
21              # If inside title...
22              if ( $intitle ) {
23                  tr/A-Za-z&;0-9/ /cs;
24                  $title .= "$_";
25              }
26              else {
27                  tr/A-Za-z&;/ /cs;
28                  foreach ( split (/ /, $_) ) {
29                      # Skip words shorter then 3 characters.
30                      next unless length($_) > 2;
31                      $freqlist{$_}++;
32                  }
33              }
34          }
35      }
36  }
```

The associative array freqlist records the number of occurrences of each word in the original file. In this example, the contents of the array are simply printed out, along with the title:

```
37  $title =~ tr/\n/ /s;
38  print ("TITLE: $title\n");
39  foreach $w (sort(keys(%freqlist))) {
40      print ("$freqlist{$w} $w\n");
41  }
```

The output is:

```
TITLE: History of the Web
1 And
1 Berners
1 CERN
1 Did
1 History
1 Lee
1 NeXT
1 Tim
2 Web
```

```
1 ago
1 browser
1 computer
1 created
...
```

The result of the text parsing process can now be fed to a database system, or stored in a simple flat file index like the <META> index file from the previous section. Of course, the parser can be refined in many ways. Acronyms such as CERN usually have a high significance, and might be indexed separately. In addition, it is possible to extract not only the title, but also headings and emphasized text.

The complete code for a Perl based free text search utility, ICE, can be found on the CDROM. As it does not use any operating system specific features it not only works under Unix, but also on Macintosh and Windows NT.

6.2   Log file Processing

By keeping track of every single HTTP connection handled by a Web server, transaction logs provide server administrators with important information. They allow the recording of client behavior, indicate which services are easily accessible and attractive, and provide a means of estimating the size of the server's remote audience. Error logs are also important, as they can indicate possible problems with the server set-up and file permissions, or highlight dangling hyperlinks which lead to non-existent documents (sometimes known as 'stale' links). Finally, some server software logs the information from the HTTP 'Referer' field (Section 2.3.3). This HTTP header field contains the URL of the document from which a request was made. By analyzing the information from this field, you can track back 'bad' links to the source. Furthermore, it provides information about how often and from where an information source has been referenced.

Utilities that analyze log files automatically and create reports are very useful both for document authors and users. In order to facilitate the creation of access log analysis tools, the server developers at CERN and NCSA agreed on a common log file format, which is used throughout our examples.

The transfer log file contains records consisting of seven space-separated fields in the format:

```
host user authuser [date:time] "request" status bytes
```

Note that *request* can have embedded spaces, and is therefore enclosed within quotation marks. Table 6.1 explains the fields and their contents.

Several sophisticated log file analysis tools already exist, some of which are mentioned in Section 6.2.3. The purpose of these programs is to generate server access statistics by counting various categories of log records. One possibility is simply to compute the total number of remote accesses on a daily or monthly basis. Using the name of the remote host, it is also possible to generate statistics on how many

Table 6.1   Log file fields

Field	Explanation
host	The DNS name or the IP number of the remote client.
user	Any information returned by *identd* for this person, or '-' otherwise.
authuser	If the user sent a user ID for authentication, this user ID, or '-' otherwise.
date	The date in the format *DD/Mon/Year*. *DD* is the two-digit day (a leading zero is provided if needed), *Mon* is the (English) abbreviation of the month name and *Year* a four-digit year (century included).
time	The time in the format *hh:mm:ss*. *hh* is the hour in 24-hour format, *mm* the minutes and *ss* the seconds. All three fields are two digits, with leading zeroes added if necessary.
request	The first line of the HTTP request as sent by the client.
status	The status code returned by the server for this request, or '-' if not available.
bytes	The total number of bytes sent (not including the HTTP header), or '-' if not available.

accesses came from a particular country, or to determine from how many distinct hosts connections were made.

Log file analysis programs typically compute statistics on such things as:

• The total number of accesses.

• The most active remote sites.

• The most frequently visited pages.

• The total volume of data transferred.

In addition, analysis tools are often used in combination with simple scripts, which perform server administration tasks such as starting the log analysis, filing away the results, and then truncating the log file in order to keep it from filling up all available disk space. Truncating a log file while the server is still running may cause problems. If the server process still has the file open, it will continue writing to the end of the log file, even after the file has been deleted or truncated by another program. This can produce strange results like log files with a large 'hole' in the middle. On a Unix system, the best way to avoid problems is as follows:

1. Rename the log file, for example using the *mv* command:

```
mv access_log access_log.old
```

Any processes in the middle of writing to the log file will be unaffected by the name change, and will continue writing to the same file, now named `access_log.old`. Note that Web servers typically use a number of log files. For example, the CERN server uses `http.log`, `http_error.log`, `http_proxy.log` and `http_cache.log`. (The CERN server can be configured to switch log files automatically every day – for details refer to the documentation for the configuration file variable `LogFileDateExt`[4].)

2. Restart or re-initialize the server. On Unix systems, this can normally be done by sending it the `SIGHUP` signal:

```
kill -HUP pid
```

where *pid* is the process ID of the Web server. After receiving the `SIGHUP` signal, the server process re-opens all its files, and creates a new log file. If the server software ignores the `SIGHUP` signal, it will be necessary to shutdown and restart the server manually. Please consult the server documentation for the best way of doing this.

3. The old log file, `access_log.old`, can now be safely compressed or deleted, with no adverse affects on the server.

In this section, we use two simple examples to demonstrate how a log file can be parsed and analyzed to create a summary report.

6.2.1 Access Statistics

The most common task performed during the generation of server transaction statistics is counting how many times a given URL or group of URLs was accessed during a specified period. Using Perl's pattern matching features, this is quite straightforward.

We use the URL and date strings as returned by the subroutine `timetolog` to construct a pattern against which every log file entry is matched. For the sake of simplicity, we have used a simple, readable search pattern in our example which is not absolutely foolproof – it could also be triggered by a strange file name that happened to match the date format.

```
1   # Get todays date in the right format.
2   ($mday, $month, $year) = &timetolog (time);
3
4   # Search pattern to match URL.
5   $url = "/~neuss/";
6
7   # Location of logfile
8   $logfile = "/usr/local/etc/httpd/logs/access_log";
9
10  $count=0;
11  open (FPIN, "<$logfile") || die ("$logfile: $!\n");
12  while ( <FPIN> ) {
13      if ( m:\[$mday/$month/$year.*"GET $url:o ) {
14          $count++;
```

---

[4]http://www.w3.org/pub/WWW/Daemon/User/Config/Overview.html

```
15        }
16   }
17
18   print ("$url was accessed $count times.\n");
```

By using the same code with just a slight modification in the search pattern, it is possible to create a monthly overview of total daily accesses. Only the 'day of the month' field needs to be replaced with the pattern '(\d\d)', which matches any two digits and stores the matched digits in the variable $1, so it can be used for indexing into the array count.

```
1    # Get todays date in the right format.
2    ($mday, $month, $year) = &timetolog (time);
3
4    # Search pattern to match URL.
5    $url = "/~neuss/";
6
7    # Location of logfile
8    $logfile = "/usr/local/etc/httpd/logs/access_log";
9
10   open (FPIN, "$logfile") || die ("$logfile: $!\n");
11   while ( <FPIN> ) {
12       if ( m:\[(\d\d)/$month/$year.*"GET $url:o ) {
13           $count[$1]++;
14       }
15   }
16
17   print ("Accesses to $url:\n");
18   foreach $i ( 1..$mday ) {
19       print ("$i/$month/$year: $count[$i]\n");
20   }
```

To present the statistics more attractively, the data can be fed into a program that generates a graph. Various libraries already exist that facilitate the task of generating graphs as GIF images. Figure 6.2 shows an example of such an automatically created image. The image was created by a statistical graph generator written by Jochen Schales. It's original purpose was to display graphically the number of registrations per day for the Third International WWW Conference. Since then, it has been significantly improved such that it can now be used as a generalized statistical graph generator. It is based on the GD graphics library[5] written in C by Thomas Boutell. The GD library provides routines to draw images quickly and write out the result as a GIF file. Both the statistics generator and the GD library (in C and Perl) are included on the CDROM.

With these tools, dynamic generation of an access graph is straightforward. All that is necessary is to generate the statistics data, specify the layout and scaling of the axes, and pass the values to the statistics generator program, which creates a GIF image of the access rates. Various options allow the layout and diagram type to be defined.

Finally, here is a programming technique that avoids having to create a separate image for every access, but still lets you keep it reasonably up to date. Whenever a call to the gateway script is being made, compare the current time with the date the statistics image was last modified. Re-create the statistics image only if a certain amount of time has elapsed. Or better still, check to see if the data to be displayed

---

[5]http://siva.cshl.org/gd/gd.html

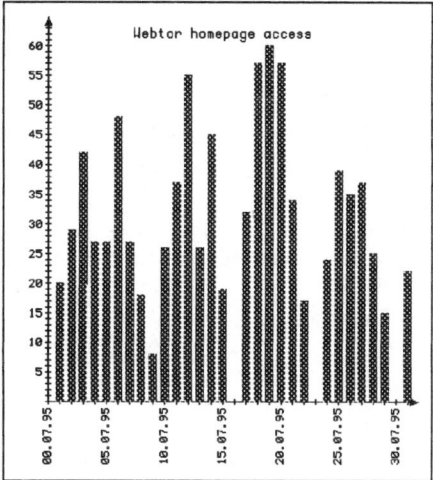

Figure 6.2   Automatically generated access graph

has changed since the image was last generated. If you make sure that the image is only generated when necessary, caching clients can avoid unnecessary transfers.

6.2.2   Automatic error reports

Current Web server technology suffers from the problem that documents are served directly from the file system, without any of the consistency mechanisms that database systems normally provide. You are probably familiar with the results – renaming a file or moving it to another place causes hyperlinks to the corresponding document to become invalid. Other problems are caused by the fact that the server program usually runs under a special user ID and thus has different access permissions to those of the user creating hypertext files. If the file permissions deny the server access to the document, every attempt to retrieve the document will result in an error.

One solution to this problem, albeit a *post hoc* one, is to run a program periodically, which analyzes the error log files and notifies the authors of documents that are causing problems.

```
1   #!/usr/local/bin/perl
2
3   # Simple error report generator.
4
5   # Open error log file for reading.
6   $errlog = "/hgdv/www/.logs/error_log";
7   open (FP, $errlog) || die ("$errlog: $!\n");
8
9   # Process it line for line.
10  while ( <FP> ) {
11      # Message: "access failed"
12      if (/\[([^]]*)\] httpd: access to (.*) fail.*reason: (.*)/) {
13          $date = $1;
14          $file = $2;
```

```
15          $reason = $3;
16          if ( -e $file
17              && $reason =~ "file permissions deny server access") {
18              &report_err ($file, $date, $reason);
19          }
20      }
21
22      # Message: "will not follow link"
23      if ( /\[(([^]]*)\] httpd: will not follow link (.*)/ ) {
24          $date = $1;
25          $file = $2;
26          $reason = "symbolic link and link destination ".
27                    "have different owners";
28          if ( -e $file ) {
29              &report_err ($file, $date, $reason);
30          }
31      }
32      # ... (add other messages here)
33  }
34
35  # Create an error report.
36  sub report_err {
37      local ($file, $date, $reason) = @_;
38
39      # Find out who owns the file...
40      local ($dev, $ino, $mode, $nlink, $uid, $gid, $rdev, $size,
41             $atime, $mtime, @dontcare) = stat ($file);
42      # ... and get the user name.
43      $user = getpwuid ($uid);
44
45      # Print a short message.
46      print ("owner:$user File:$file Error:$reason\n");
47  }
```

Of course, instead of just printing out a report, it is also possible to send an automatic email message to the file owner. However, it is important not to bombard individual users with hundreds of automatic reports. By collecting messages for individual users and sending each user a summary report on their files, the number of outgoing messages can be limited. The complete code of an error log parser which sends error reports as email messages by connecting to the *sendmail* program is included in the appendix (Section A.2.1).

6.2.3   Other statistics gatherers

For those who decide not to build their own access statistics gathering tool, but rather to use an existing package, here are some that might be of interest:

getstats
A fully featured log analyzer written in C by Kevin Hughes of EIT. Available from: http://www.eit.com/software/getstats/getstats.html.

WWWstat
Another fully featured log analyzer, written in Perl by Roy Fielding at the University of California, Irvine.
Available from http://www.ics.uci.edu/WebSoft/wwwstat/.

wusage
An analyzer that can create GIF statistics charts, written in C by Thomas Boutell, when he was with the Quest Center at Cold Spring Harbor Labs.
Available from http://siva.cshl.org/wusage.html.

6.3   Converting foreign formats

Conducting any kind of business relies heavily on communication. Of course this includes communication between customers and business partners, but efficient and timely communication between colleagues is also of vital importance. Electronic mail systems and the Internet in general have greatly facilitated this task. The World Wide Web was designed as a corporate information system, a tool for structuring and accessing information. Not only can hypertext documents be distributed electronically, it is also possible to provide access to various external information sources by means of gateway programs.

If these information sources are in a format that is not directly digestible for Web browsers, for example a corporate database, the foreign format has to be converted to HTML first. This cannot always be done by creating static files and placing them in a directory. One reason might be that the information itself is not static, but is generated dynamically, for example by querying a database system. Alternatively the amount of information might be so vast that duplicating it would be undesirable. A gateway program can perform tasks such as converting a foreign format or providing a searchable index for the underlying information source. The examples in this section cover automatic format converters, and the creation of searchable indexes and hyperlinked structures.

6.3.1   Indexing mailboxes

More and more corporations are beginning to make use of electronic mail as a means of communicating with customers. Since communication takes place electronically, it is easy to maintain a record of interactions and keep track of the messages exchanged with a specific customer. To provide a marketing and sales department with an information system that allows for various searches and operations on recorded mail messages, a Web gateway to an email archive can be created. This section provides a simple gateway to search a mailbox archive. It can easily be enhanced with features such as tagging messages as 'processed', or tacking an annotation to a given message in the form of a hyperlink.

Search mail archive

Search field: ░░░░░░░ for expression: [.............]

░░░░░░

Figure 6.3   Searching a mail archive: the forms front-end

Search result

From: "squirrel@crl.com"
Date: Mon, 30 Jan 1995 13:12:52 -0800 (PST)
Subject: Re: WWW 95 info

From: rob@bedazzled.com
Date: Mon, 30 Jan 1995 23:57:06 -0500 (EST)
Subject: Re: WWW Article

From: Daniel J. Gamble
Date: Tue, 31 Jan 95 11:57:47 -0700
Subject: Re: Canon Observation

Figure 6.4   Searching a mail archive: search result

Most mail readers store messages simply by concatenating the mail messages and their corresponding headers into a single file. When creating a Web gateway to search and access a mailbox, performance can become a critical issue. A mailbox file can easily grow to several megabytes in size. To allow for fast searches on its contents or on specific header fields such as subject or sender, a pre-computed index into the file should be maintained.

The principle of this approach is quite simple. A parser breaks down the file contents into its constituent parts and creates a list of attribute–value pairs, which represent the information extracted by the parser. By storing these pairs in a separate index file, look-ups can be performed much faster than by searching the whole file in a linear fashion. After identifying the messages that fulfill a search condition, another routine can extract them. By inserting HTML tags, mail headers can be highlighted, and URLs contained in the mail body can be converted to functioning hyperlinks.

This section demonstrates how a simple searchable mail archive can be created by indexing mail headers. Figure 6.5 shows the format of information contained in the index.

$From_1$	$Subject_1$	$Date_1$	$Position_1$
$From_2$	$Subject_2$	$Date_2$	$Position_2$
$\vdots$	$\vdots$	$\vdots$	$\vdots$
$From_n$	$Subject_n$	$Date_n$	$Position_n$

Figure 6.5   A simple index to access mailbox files

After the parser has extracted the relevant mail header fields, they are stored in the index file, together with the file position at which the mail message starts (this will be needed later for the efficient retrieval of individual messages). The fields can be separated using a character that does not appear in any of the fields, such as a tab.

A Web gateway program that uses this index file for searching the mailbox contents can perform pattern matching on one of the header fields and build up a list of positions. These positions can be used to construct URLs that point to the same gateway program, but with the position information attached to the URL as described in Section 4.1. Selecting one of these URLs then invokes the gateway program, instructing it to extract the corresponding mail message, convert it to hypertext, and pass it to the Web client.

Following the example given in Section 5.5, the initial forms generation, the searching and the dynamic extraction processes can all be handled by a single gateway program. Which of the three tasks it should perform can be determined by analyzing the query:

- If no query data is provided, the program should generate the HTML code for the form.

- If query data is supplied for *subject*, *from*, or *date*, it should search for the string specified, and generate a list of URLs leading to the corresponding mail messages. Such a URL consists of the URL path leading to the program itself (as available from the environment variable SCRIPT_NAME), with a question mark followed by position=*num* appended to it (Section 4.1).

- If query data is supplied for *position*, it should extract the mail message that starts at the given file position, convert it to hypertext format, and return it.

Firstly, the index of the mailbox headers must be generated. Since the index file format selected is very simple, creating the index is not difficult. The indexing program simply needs to distinguish between mail header and body, extract the From, Date, and Subject fields, and store them, along with the message's file position, in the index file.

```
1   #!/usr/local/bin/perl
2
3   # Create a simple index from a file in mailbox format. Set the
4   # $MAILFILE and $INDEXFILE variables to point to the mailbox file
5   # resp. the index file you want to create.
6
7   $MAILFILE = "tmp.mbox";
8   $INDEXFILE = "tmp.idx";
9
10  local ($isinheader);
11
12  # Open Mailbox and index file.
13  open (FPIN, "$MAILFILE") || die ("$MAILFILE: $!\n");
14  open (FPOUT, ">$INDEXFILE") || die ("$INDEXFILE: $!\n");
15
16  while ( <FPIN> ) {
17      if ( $isinheader ) {
18          # Parse the mail header and store the values.
19          if ( /^Date: (.*)$/ ){
20              ($date = $1) =~ tr/\t/ /s;
21          }
22          if ( /^Subject: (.*)$/ ) {
23              ($subject = $1) =~ tr/\t/ /s;
24          }
25          if ( /^From: (.*)$/ ) {
26              ($from = $1) =~ tr/\t/ /s;
27          }
```

```
28            if( /^$/ ){  # empty line ends the header
29                $isinheader = 0;
30                # Write out header values to index file
31                # and reset them.
32                print FPOUT ("$pos\t$from\t$date\t$subject\n");
33                $date = $subject = $from = $pos = "";
34            }
35        }
36        else {
37            if ( /^From (.*)$/ ) {
38                # "From " starts next mail header.
39                # Get current position.
40                $pos = tell (FPIN);
41                $isinheader = 1;
42            }
43        }
44    }
45    close (FPIN);
46    close (FPOUT);
```

Figure 6.3 shows the forms interface as generated by the gateway program described below. The user can select a mail header field to search, and enter a search expression to match against.

```
1   #!/usr/local/bin/perl
2
3   # Install this script in your servers CGI directory, and
4   # set the $MAILFILE and $INDEXFILE variables to point to the
5   # Mailbox you're searching resp. the mail header index for this
6   # mailbox file. Use "indexmail.pl" to create the index.
7
8   $MAILFILE = "tmp.mbox";
9   $INDEXFILE = "tmp.idx";
10
11  # Send the HTTP header
12  &send_header();
13
14  # Do the real work, trapping any errors.
15  eval { &main; };
16
17  # If an error has occured, log it to STDOUT.
18  if ( $@ ) {
19      &html_start ("Error in Script");
20      print ("$@\n");
21      &html_end;
22      exit;
23  }
24
25  # Main routine.
26  #
27  # If no forms input is available, send the form
28  # otherwise decode forms input and execute search.
29  sub main {
30      # If content_length is zero and query string is empty.
31      if ( ($ENV{'CONTENT_LENGTH'} == 0) &&
32           (length($ENV{'QUERY_STRING'}) == 0) ) {
33          # We're not decoding a form yet => send the form .
34          &html_start ("Search mail archive");
35          &send_index ();
36          return;
37      }
38      &html_start ("Search results");
39
40      # Parse forms result and store it in an associative array .
41      %forms = &cgiparse ();
```

If the user enters data in the forms interface shown in Figure 6.3 and performs a query by selecting the 'Search' button, the field values are encoded into a query string and sent to the the server, whereupon the gateway program decodes its input by calling cgiparse, and stores the result into an associative array. The functions html_start and html_end provide a wrapper which complies to the CGI specification and the HTML standard. These routines are described in Section 5.2.2.

By examining the parameters from the forms interface, we can distinguish between a header search and a request for a single message:

```
42      # Depending on how this script has been invoked, either
43      # search the mail header index file or extract a specific
44      # mail article from the mailbox.
45      if ( defined $forms{"Field"} ) {
46          # "Field" provided => search mail header.
47          print (&searchheader($forms{"Expr"}, $forms{"Field"}));
48      }
49      elsif ( defined $forms{"Position"} ) {
50          # "Position" provided => extract mail message.
51          print (&extractmail($forms{"Position"}));
52      }
53      else {
54          # This is an "I shouldn't be here" error.
55          print ("Internal error:  wrong forms frontend?\n");
56      }
57
58      print ("</BODY>");
59      return;
60   }
```

Generating the HTML text for the form is straightforward. It consists of a selection field containing options for each mail header, and a text input field for the search expression.

```
61   # Display the Forms interface.
62   sub send_index {
63       local ($scriptname) = $ENV{"SCRIPT_NAME"};
64       print ("<FORM $method ACTION=\"$scriptname\">\n");
65
66       print <<"ENDHTML";
67   <P>
68   Search field:
69   <SELECT NAME="Field">
70   <OPTION>      Subject
71   <OPTION>      From
72   <OPTION>      Date
73   </SELECT>
74   for expression: <INPUT NAME="Expr"  SIZE=10>
75   <P>
76   <INPUT TYPE="submit" VALUE="Search..">
77   <HR></BODY>
78   ENDHTML
79   }
```

The most straightforward method of searching the index file is to work through it line by line and compare the search expression against the appropriate header field entry. Perl's pattern matching features make this task fairly simple. First the input parameters are parsed in order to determine which header field is to be examined, then the complete index file is read into an array.

Pre-compiled search expressions have quite an impact on search performance. By pre-compiling the search expression, the following `grep` command can compute a list of all index lines containing the search expression very efficiently.

```
80   # Search the index file for a given expression.
81   sub searchheader {
82       local ($expr, $field) = @_;
83       local ($num, $result);
84       $scriptname = $ENV{"SCRIPT_NAME"};
85
86       # Determine which field in the mail header.
87       $num = 0;
88       if ($field eq "From")    { $num=1 };
89       if ($field eq "Date")    { $num=2 };
90       if ($field eq "Subject") { $num=3 };
91
92       if ( $num == 0 ) {
93           # "I shouldn't be here" error.
94           $result .= "Internal error:  wrong forms frontend?\n";
95           $result .= "The item 'Field' had the unknown value ".
96                         "[$field]\n";
97           return $result;
98       }
99
100      # Open index and read it into an array.
101      open (FP, "$INDEXFILE") || die ("$INDEXFILE: $!\n");
102      @dbase = <FP>;
103      close (FP);
104
105      # 1. Search for expression in the whole header (fast).
106      $expr =~ /$expr/i;    # pre-compile search regexp
107      @result = grep (//i, @dbase);
```

The next step is to take the result from the previous pattern match, split it into the seperate header fields, and compare the field specified in the `field` parameter with the search expression. If a match is detected, a URL describing the match is constructed and stored in `result`. Since the mail messages do not exist as separate HTML files but must be extracted dynamically, this URL must also point to a gateway program. By using the `SCRIPT_NAME` environment variable, we construct a URL that points to the same gateway program, but contains an additional parameter `Postion=num`, where *num* is the file position at which the matching mail message starts.

```
108      foreach $i ( @result ) {
109          # 2. Split into the seperate fields...
110          @vec = split (/\t|\n/, $i);
111          # ...and compare again.
112          if ( $vec[$num] =~ // ) {
113              ($pos, $from, $date, $subject) = @vec;
114              $result .= "<B>From</B>: $from <BR>\n";
115              $result .= "<B>Date</B>: $date <BR>\n";
116              # Create link to dynamically extract message.
117              unless ( $subject ) {
118                  $subject = "(NO SUBJECT)";
119              }
120              $result .= "<B>Subject</B>: \n";
121              $result .= "<A HREF=\"$scriptname?Position=$pos\">\n";
122              $result .= "<I>$subject</I></A><P>\n";
123          }
124      }
125      $result;
126  }
```

If the user selects one of these dynamically created URLs, the main routine calls the function extractmail. Extracting a single mail message is achieved by seeking to the appropriate position in the mailbox file, and then printing out every line until the start of the next message or the end of the file is encountered. The start of the next message can be found by looking for a line beginning with 'From ' (that is 'From' followed by a space). This is a convention used by many mail reading programs, although it will cause confusion when a line starting with 'From ' appears in the body of a mail message. For this reason, mail handling programs usually quote such lines by preceding them with the '>' character.

Until the beginning of the next message is found, the current line is passed through a simple filter that converts the special characters '<', '>' and '&' to the equivalent HTML replacement strings. Then, by looking for a pattern that describes the format of URLs, embedded hyperlinks are converted into a 'clickable' form. After adding a <BR> tag in order to create a new line in the browser, the resulting HTML text is concatenated and returned to the caller.

```
127   # Extract the mail message starting at the byte offset "pos".
128   sub extractmail {
129       local ($pos) = @_;
130       local ($result);
131
132       # Open Mailbox file for reading.
133       unless ( open (FPIN, "$MAILFILE") ) {
134           $result = "<PRE>cannot read file \"$MAILFILE\"</PRE>\n";
135           return $result;
136       }
137
138       # Move to absolute position $pos.
139       seek (FPIN, $pos, 0);
140
141       # Turn it into hypertext.
142       while ( <FPIN> ) {
143           if ( /^From (.*)$/ ) {
144               # "From " starts next mail header.
145               last; # end of while loop
146           }
147           else {
148               # Protect against HTML special characters.
149               s|&|&amp;|;
150               s|<|&lt;|;
151               s|>|&gt;|;
152               # Turn URLs into hyperlinks.
153               s|(http:[\w/.:+\-~%]+)|<A HREF="$&">$&</A>|g;
154               $result .= "$_<BR>";
155           }
156       }
157       close FPIN;
158       $result;
159   }
```

Of course, this gateway program is very simple. It does not provide a search facility for the mail body, neither does it thread messages that are replies to a previous mail message (the latter feature is extremely useful for converting the discussion in a mailing list to a hypertext archive). In order to create a more sophisticated gateway program, you can either work from the code provided with this book to create your own indexing tool, or install mail indexing software from the public domain.

One mail indexing tool worth looking at is Hypermail[6], which was originally developed and designed by Tom Gruber for Enterprise Integration Technologies (EIT) in Common Lisp, and later rewritten in C by Kevin Hughes (also at EIT). Its indexing routine will convert references in each message to email addresses and URLs to hyperlinks so they can be selected. In addition, Hypermail also keeps track of threads and creates links to the previous and next message in the thread.

6.3.2   Indexing electronic news

The Usenet system for the distribution of electronic news was among the earliest information services on the Internet, and provides people all over the world with a 'bulletin board' type of system, which is similar to services such as those provided by Compuserve or America Online, but with a much larger audience. Like the World Wide Web, Usenet has no centralized structure: articles can originate at any site and are distributed world-wide by the Usenet software.

Electronic news can be accessed by any site that has either a UUCP (Unix to Unix Copy) connection or full IP (Internet Protocol) network connectivity. In the case of an IP connection, the protocol used is the *Network News Transfer Protocol* (NNTP), a protocol for transferring news articles between sites.

News articles are organized into newsgroups, dedicated to specific topics. Usenet carries a vast amount of information and keeping up to date with even a small subset of the 5,000 or more different groups can be very time consuming. A Web gateway to electronic news can provide an access method with added searching facilities. This section provides a very simple interface to Usenet news articles.

Parsing of articles is easy if access to the Usenet server's file hierarchy is available (normally, news files reside under `/usr/spool/news`, conveniently called the 'news spool'). Direct file access to the news articles avoids having to use the NNTP protocol to retrieve articles, which can be complicated and time consuming. Indexing the spool files can be done on a file by file basis, using the same mechanism that we described in Section 6.3.1. However, modern news systems have a feature called OVERVIEW, which provides an index file that resides in the news spool, and is updated by the news software itself. Using the OVERVIEW index file, a relatively simple program can produce an HTML file with 'clickable' Hyperlinks. Since the index file is updated by the news software itself, there is no need for regular updates of a separate index file.

Here is the source code for an OVERVIEW based program that produces a list of Usenet articles as hypertext. It is very fast, taking only a couple of seconds to convert a large newsgroup of several thousand articles.

```
1  #!/usr/local/bin/perl
2
3  # This program reads a USEnet news .overview file and outputs an
4  # HTML document with article references.
5  #
```

---

[6]http://www.eit.com/software/hypermail/hypermail.html

```
6    # One argument: the newsgroup.
7
8    # Get newsgroup name.
9    $group = shift (@ARGV);
10   # Turn it into a file name.
11   ($groupf = $group) =~ s/\./\//g;
12
13   # Open the overview file.
14   open (OV, "/usr/spool/news/$groupf/.overview")
15       || die ("/usr/spool/news/$groupf/.overview: $!\n");
16
17   # HTML headings.
18   &html_start ("Newsgroup: $group");
19
20   # Start of list.
21   print STDOUT ("<ol>\n",
22                 "<lh>Newsgroup: $group</lh>\n");
23
24   # Process the overview file.
25   while ( <OV> ) {
26
27       ($artno, $subject, $author, $date, $msgid, $refs,
28        $bytes, $lines) = split (/\t/);
29
30       # Protect against HTML special characters.
31       $subject = &html_encode ($subject);
32       $author = &html_encode ($author);
33       $msgid = &html_encode ($msgid);
34
35       # Write index line.
36       print STDOUT ("<li sequence=$artno><a\n",
37                     "href=\"news:$msgid\">",
38                     "<b>$subject</b></a>\n",
39                     "   <i>$author</i>, $bytes bytes.\n");
40   }
41   # End the list.
42   print STDOUT ("</ol>\n");
43
44   # HTML trailer
45   &html_end;
46
47   # Subroutines
48
49   sub html_encode {
50       local ($s) = @_;
51       $s =~ s/&/&amp;/g;
52       $s =~ s/</&lt;/g;
53       $s =~ s/>/&gt;/g;
54       $s =~ s/"/&quot;/g;
55       $s;
56   }
```

This program could be improved in various ways, for instance by providing a dynamic hyperlink to a gateway routine, which recognizes embedded URLs and converts them into hyperlinks, using the same approach as in Section 6.3.1. However, an increasing number of Web browsers include this functionality with their news-reading code. They use a special URL scheme 'news' for this purpose.

Another enhancement might be the creation of a pre-computed index in order to speed up access. This is not very difficult. The converter simply needs to compare the date of the OVERVIEW file and the pre-computed index. If the index file is up to date, it is passed on to the client; otherwise, it is rebuilt before being returned.

Finally, instead of presenting the article headers as links to newsgroup articles, an indexing tool can parse the contents of the articles and create an archive that provides free text searches into newsgroup articles.

6.4   Relational databases

A corporate information system must feature a data repository for organizing and storing information in a consistent way. Although object oriented database systems are much discussed when it comes to data repositories, they are not yet widely used. A much larger body of information is stored in industry-standard relational databases.

Web gateways to database systems can not only make information available to clients in a wide area network, but also provide a much friendlier interface for users within a corporation. Using the CGI standard for server gateways, an information request from a forms interface can be translated into one or more SQL queries, which are executed by the database system. The output from the query can be post-processed if necessary, and formatted using HTML markup.

This section shows how a simple but powerful gateway can be created by calling an SQL interpreter from within a Perl program. Since relational database operations are typically text oriented, Perl is well-suited to this task. Using Perl gateway programs that interface to a relational database system, you can create database applications accessible via the World Wide Web.

6.4.1   Creating an SQL gateway

A database is a collection of information, just like any flat-file based information system. What differentiates it is that the database provides a number of additional features which help to maintain data consistency and facilitate the identification and accessing of relevant information. These features include:

- *Concurrency*
  Multiple users can query and modify a database simultaneously, while the database server ensures that the accesses are performed in sequence avoiding conflicts.

- *Access control*
  The database system can restrict read and write access to certain items.

- *Transaction management*
  A series of database operations can be grouped together to form a *transaction*. All operations in a transaction are guaranteed to have been accomplished successfully when the transaction is completed. If any one of the operations fails, the database is 'rolled back' (restored) to the state it was in before the start of the transaction.

Most database systems used in the industry follow the relational model devised by E.F. Codd [Codd70]. Data is stored in the form of tables comprising rows and columns. Each column represents an attribute, each row an instance described in the table. Table 6.2 shows a simple table representing information from an employee database.

Table 6.2 A simple employee database table

ID	LastName	FirstName	Phone	Mgr.
E1578	Algar	Garth	141	E2890
E1542	Campbell	Wayne	199	E2890
E3520	Smith	Kevin	131	E1542
E2890	Patel	Hanif	254	
E2893	Smith	Jane	255	

The standard language used for accessing relational database systems is *Structured Query Language* (SQL), a brief example of which is given here. In order to retrieve data from the database system, a SELECT statement is issued containing a FROM clause which specifies the table(s) to be accessed, and a WHERE clause containing a search condition. For example, in the table shown, the SQL statement

```
SELECT ID, Phone
  FROM employee
  WHERE LastName = 'Smith'
```

retrieves the ID and phone extension of all employees with the last name 'Smith'.

The SQL standard was issued in 1986 by the American National Standards Institute (ANSI), it defines a core set of SQL features. Database vendors usually define extensions to the SQL core set. For a detailed description of the specific SQL flavor your database system implements, consult its manuals.

There are several ways in which you can create an SQL gateway. The most straight-forward solution is to start up an SQL interpreter from within the gateway program and issue SQL statements by piping them to the interpreter's standard input, which is how the following short Perl program operates.

First the environment variables required by the interpreter are set. These settings are, of course, highly system dependent.

```
1  #!/usr/local/bin/perl
2
3  # Environment settings.
4  $ENV{"ORACLE_SID"} = "oracle6";
5  $ENV{"ORACLE_HOME"} = "/a3db1/oracle6";
6
7  # Path to sql interpreter, arguments to pass it.
8  $sqlplus = "/a3db1/oracle6/bin/sqlplus";
9  $sqlargs = "-s www95/wp5";
```

Then, an SQL statement to retrieve the data from the database is defined. Again, there are various settings (lines 13–18) that are system dependent. These settings control the interpreter's behavior rather then defining a statement to access data. More then one select statement can be executed in a single script.

```
10   # Sqlcommands to execute.
11   $sqlcommands = <<'END';
12     whenever sqlerror exit sql.sqlcode none;
13     set flush off;
14     set feedback off;
15     set echo off;
16     set showmode off;
17     set heading off;
18     set verify off;
19
20     select 'Conference Registered:     '||count(*)·
21     from chris.www_reg
22     where conference = 'R' and cancel_date is null;
23
24     select 'Conference Waitlisted:     '||count(*)
25     from chris.www_reg
26     where conference = 'W' and cancel_date is null;
27
28     select 'Developer Day Registered: '||count(*)
29     from chris.www_reg
30     where develop = 'R' and cancel_date is null;
31
32     select 'Developer Day Waitlisted: '||count(*)
33     from chris.www_reg
34     where develop = 'W' and cancel_date is null;
35   END
```

Finally, the interpreter is executed by opening a pipe, and the SQL data is fed to the process's standard input.

```
36   # Open pipe to sql interpreter...
37   open (FP, "| $sqlplus $sqlargs") ||
38       die ("couldn't open pipe to sql interpreter: $!\n");
39
40   # ..and pass sql statements to it.
41   print FP ($sqlcommands);
42
43   # Close it.
44   close(FP);
```

The result is printed to the standard output, and looks like this:

```
Conference Registered:     956
Conference Waitlisted:     0
Developer Day Registered: 300
Developer Day Waitlisted: 0
```

By post-processing the data returned from the interpreter, a gateway program can produce nicely formatted HTML output. Figure 6.6 shows a page used for the Third International World-Wide Web Conference. It was dynamically generated by accessing a database system with registration information.

In order to access the data returned from the interpreter, it is possible to redirect the output to a file and read the data from there:

```
$outfile = "/some/path";
open (FP, "| $sqlplus $sqlargs > $outfile") ||
    die ("couldn't open pipe to SQL interpreter: $!\n");
```

It is also possible to read the data returned from the interpreter directly, although this can be slightly awkward. The problem is that a pipe is needed both to and from the sub-process. Although this is possible, it can lead to deadlock situations.

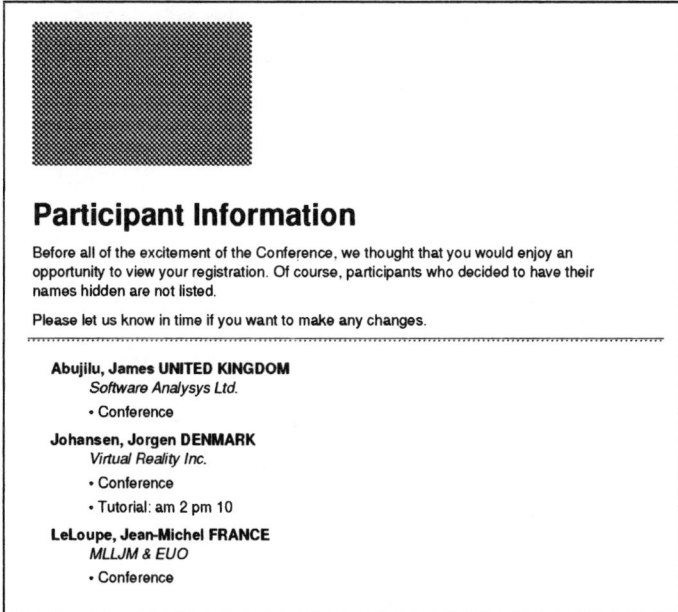

Figure 6.6   Database interface: Participant Information

Imagine that the program sends something via the pipe to the interpreter process and awaits a response. That process, however, is not satisfied with the supplied input and requires some more input. Now both processes will wait for each other indefinitely. A safe way around this is to spawn a separate process which calls the interpreter and feeds data to it. The output of that process can then be read via another pipe by the original (parent) process.

In Perl, this can be done quite elegantly using the special filehandle '- |'. It creates a child process with its output connected to an open pipe to the parent. Before forking off the child process, we must flush any data left in the output buffer.

```
# Unbuffer stdout before forking and flush it.
select((select(STDOUT),$|=1)[0]) ;
print ("");

$pid = open (FPIPE, "-|");
# Child process: call SQL interpreter.
if( $pid == 0 ) {
    ... # call sql interpreter and feed input to it
    exit;
}

# Parent process: post-process results.
while ( <FPIPE> ) {
    ... # process inout
  }
```

Section A.3.1 contains sample code for a database interface using this technique. Its application is not limited to database interfaces. All sorts of gateways can be created by programming a 'wrapper' around an interpreter. The advantage of this approach is that it does not require any kind of interface library or modification to the Perl interpreter. One disadvantage is that only rudimentary error handling can be performed, but the main drawback is that on every access to the gateway the SQL interpreter is started up and a new connection to the database must be established (including authorization). This can be time consuming.

An alternative approach involves providing the gateway program with an embedded interface to SQL. The *Perl common database interface* (DBperl) provides a higher level interface which facilitates the writing of queries in a database-independent way. By compiling an extension into the Perl interpreter, the programmer is provided with a standardized set of SQL based Perl function extensions, such as db_fetch and db_attach, for manipulating relational databases.

The official archive for the DBperl extensions is ftp.demon.co.uk[7]. It contains copies of ports for a variety of database engines including Sybase, Oracle, Ingres, Informix, and Interbase.

6.4.2   Queries via fill-out forms

The fill-out form user interface provided by most Web browsers can be used to communicate with a database system, thus providing a graphical user interface (GUI), which is economical, both in terms of money and programming effort, for existing corporate information systems. The casual user can use simple fill-out forms interfaces instead of having to learn a query language. Furthermore, creating a forms driven gateway to a database can make the information available on a world-wide scale, without the information provider having to distribute (let alone pay for) special software or libraries for the remote database access.

In order to create a forms based interface to a database system, some problems caused by the design of the HTTP protocol need to be overcome:

- HTTP only allows for stateless connections. Starting a new database session for every incoming request can be quite time-consuming.

- Since HTTP does not implement the concept of a session with multiple operations related to each other, it is not possible to use the transaction mechanism to ensure data consistency.

- Information from a previous interaction cannot be re-used, for example to provide a *virtual shopping cart* mechanism where you visit a forms page to pick up some items, go to the next page to add some more, and so on.

The lack of a stateful transaction is the biggest obstacle to using Web forms interfaces for database access. Future versions of HTTP will address this problem by supporting virtual sessions. However, stateful transactions can also be provided using the current version of HTTP, in one of two ways:

---

[7]ftp://ftp.demon.co.uk/pub/perl/db

1. By encoding additional information into the URL that refers to the gateway program.

2. By storing the information in hidden fields in the forms interface (Section 3.5.1).

For the first method the gateway program keeps track of the clients operations, and encodes some kind of 'customer identifier' in the URL. For example, on the 'Welcome Page' the customer might be asked to enter certain data, before being allowed access to the information system. This could be information such as a name, email address, or a registration number obtained during a previous visit. This is not required for creating a unique transaction identifier, but might be necessary in case some kind of authentication is required.

On submitting the form, the gateway program associated with the form generates a unique identifier and encodes it into the URL in the ACTION attribute of the FORM element (Section 3.5.1). If for example,

```
http://www.your.site/cgi-bin/eval-form
```

leads to the gateway program that decodes the form, appending a unique identifier to the URL, like this:

```
http://www.your.site/cgi-bin/eval-form/id0815
```

makes this string available to the gateway program via the PATH_INFO environment variable (Section 4.3).

The gateway program that handles the form also decodes the input and performs the requested actions. Using the transaction identifier obtained from the URL, the gateway program logs the operations performed by the client (thus providing a virtual shopping cart). The form is generated as the program's output, and the transaction identifier encoded as before.

When the whole transaction is completed, the identifier can be used to obtain the complete list of operations the client has performed. After a *log off* operation, the transaction log can be discarded. The same should be done if a certain timeout threshold has been reached without further action from the client.

For the second method, the same effect is achieved in a more convenient way by storing state information in a hidden field of fill-out forms:

```
<FORM   ...>
<INPUT TYPE="hidden" NAME="ID" VALUE="0815">
</FORM>
```

Provided that the POST method is used, hidden form fields do not suffer from the drawbacks of URL (that the length of the encoded data must not exceed limits in the client or server side software). Thus, instead of storing transaction information and tagging it with a unique identifier, the complete information can be stored in a set of hidden fields, for example:

```
<FORM   ...>
<INPUT TYPE="hidden" NAME="item1" VALUE="details of book ordered">
<INPUT TYPE="hidden" NAME="item2" VALUE="second book">
<INPUT TYPE="hidden" NAME="item3" VALUE="and another one">

...
</FORM>
```

Hidden fields are easy to decode; they are encoded by the client exactly like the normal, 'visible' forms items.

Further information on preserving state information across HTTP requests is covered in Section 7.4.

7

Electronic Transactions

In Section 5.5 we described a program that performs a basic transaction by appending a couple of lines of information to a local file. For real life applications this is not generally sufficient. In this chapter we discuss what is needed to perform more complicated transactions.

7.1   Validating input

While writing gateway programs one has to keep in mind that the Web operates according to the client–server model of processing. The gateway programs are just back-ends for the server. More importantly, the client–server connection is extremely open. There is not the slightest guarantee that the data passed to the gateway program by the server was generated by the client expected. Any user can write his or her own fill-out form and make it send arbitrary data to your server and thus to your gateway program; therefore the validation of input data is crucial.

It is a good habit to adopt a defensive strategy when processing data that originates from a questionable source. Never assume that a certain field contains a specific value just because your fill-out form has set it up that way. The following guidelines should be applied to gateway programs:

- All input data should be thoroughly validated, before it is stored or otherwise processed.

- The program should be designed to cope with any input data, no matter how unexpected, without crashing.

- Depending on circumstances, it may be considered desirable to reject any invalid input data.

There are no general rules for validating all types of input. The following sections describe a number of common cases that can easily be adapted to suit specific needs.

7.1.1   Validating numbers

Positive integer numbers can easily be validated by testing with the following Perl pattern:

```
$num =~ /^\+?\d+$/
```

This pattern permits a leading plus sign, but leading or trailing spaces will cause the match to fail. Should they be allowed, the pattern becomes:

```
$num =~ /^\s*\+?\d+\s*$/
```

Do not omit the pattern anchors '^' and '$' since omission would render the pattern useless.

For general integers, which can take positive as well as negative values, the pattern becomes:

```
$num =~ /^\[-+]?\d+$/
```

Note that a '-' in a character class is used to denote a range of characters, except when it immediately follows the opening bracket.

The above patterns do not detect number strings that are too long. To limit the match to a certain number of digits, for example 4, use:

```
$num =~ /^\+?\d{1,4}$/
```

This can be combined with a range check:

```
$num =~ /^\+?\d{1,4}$/ && $num >= 1900 && $num <= 1995
```

A final example matches a number with an optional fractional part, which may be useful in validating financial applications. It rejects degenerate cases like '+.12'.

```
$num =~ /^[-+]?\d{1,12}(\.\d{0,4})?$/
```

7.1.2   Validating dates

Validating dates can be a painful task, since there are so many different ways to represent them. The first step therefore is to limit the allowable representations. For example, '1995/09/24' is an unambiguous way to represent Sunday September 24, 1995. But '10/11/12' could mean November 12, 1910 (or 2010!) as well as November 10, 1912 or October 11, 1912 or December 11, 1910. Usually it is enough to enter a comment on the fill-out form such as:

```
Enter the date of birth in the format YYYY/MM/DD, e.g. 1954/07/24
```

The following code performs simple validation for a date entered in this format:

```
if ( $date =~ m'^(\d\d\d\d)/(\d\d)/(\d\d)$' ) {
    $year = $1;
    $month = $2;
    $day = $3;
    $okay = ($month >= 1 && $month <= 12)
            && ($day >= 1 && $day <= 31);
}
```

The code could be improved by making the highest allowable day number dependent on the month. Depending on the application, additional constraints can often be applied to the year. When dealing with the birth date of a living person, sensible limits can be determined by considering an appropriate (and possible) range of ages.

7.1.3   Using tables to validate text

If a specific input field should contain one of a limited number of possibilities, it can easily be validated using an associative array:

```
$okay = defined $table{$entry}
```

The array can be filled by the gateway program itself, for example:

```
%table = ( 'January', 1,
           'February', 1,
           'March', 1,
           ...
         );
```

Note that the value associated with the key is immaterial. Only the presence of the key is relevant. Larger tables are better stored on disk as a DBM file, a single-key indexed file supported on most Unix systems. This file must be opened with a suitable dbmopen statement, and can then be treated just like any other associative array:

```
dbmopen (%table, $tablefile, 0666);
$okay = defined $table{$entry};
```

This approach is especially useful for checking access codes, zip codes, phone numbers and so on. Of course, the table or DBM file could contain significant values and also be used to translate the entry text to an internal representation suitable for further processing:

```
%table = ( 'January', 1,
           'February', 2,
           'March', 3,
           ...
         );
```

7.2   Handling concurrency

When two or more processes attempt to modify the same data files, concurrency control is needed to prevent information from getting lost or corrupted. This is especially true for data in ordinary files since most systems, other than relational database systems, do not provide automatic concurrency control.

7.2.1   Example: a virtual guest book

In this section, we use the file locking technique described in Section 5.2.4 to implement a simple virtual guest book which allows a user to give his or her name, address, and URL. The information is stored in a file, and on request provides users with a formatted list of guests. Figure 7.1 shows the introductory screen of the virtual guest book.

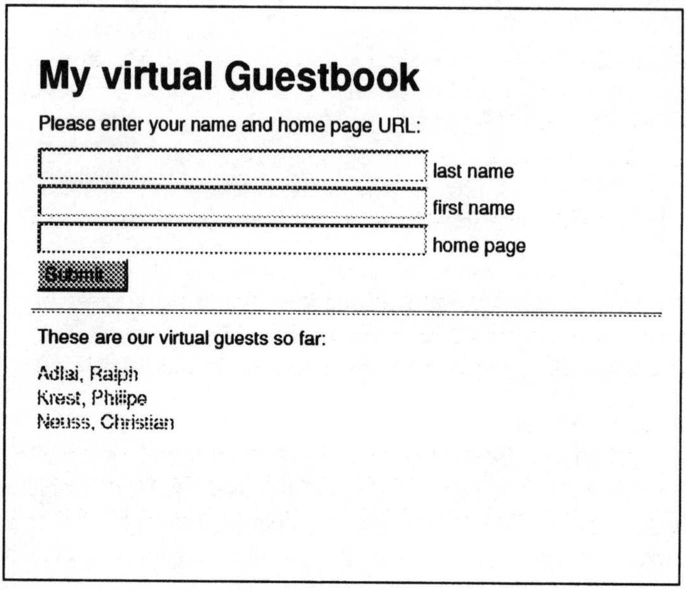

My virtual Guestbook

Please enter your name and home page URL:

_____ last name
_____ first name
_____ home page

Submit

These are our virtual guests so far:

Adlai, Ralph
Krest, Philipe
Neuss, Christian

Figure 7.1   Virtual guest book

The code for such a guest book is quite simple. As usual, a routine to trap errors is set up, and then the forms input is decoded.

```
1  #!/usr/local/bin/perl
2
3  # Where to store the guestbook:
4  $GUESTFILE = "/igd/a3/home1/neuss/tmp/guest";
5
6  &send_header ();
7
8  # Do the real work, trapping any errors.
9  eval { &main; };
10
11 # If an error has occured, log it to STDOUT.
12 if ( $@ ) {
13     &html_start ("Error in Script");
14     print STDOUT ("$@\n");
15     &html_end;
16     exit;
17 }
18
19 sub main{
20     # Send HTML header.
21     &html_start ("My Virtual Guest Book");
22
23     # Do we have input?
24     if ( $ENV{'CONTENT_LENGTH'} == 0 &&
25         $ENV{'QUERY_STRING'} eq '' ) {
26         # Send the input form.
27         &send_form ();
28         return;
29     }
30
```

```
31    # Parse forms result and store it in an associative array.
32    %forms = &cgiparse ();
33
34    $lastname = $forms{"lastname"};
35    $firstname = $forms{"firstname"};
36    $url = $forms{"url"};
```

The guest book file is locked for exclusive access, and the data that was gathered from the forms front-end is appended. Please note that, for the sake of brevity, error or consistency checks were omitted. For a 'real life' application, these must of course be incorporated, otherwise users of your guest book can create various 'enhancements' to your guest book layout. One of the funniest Web pranks we have come across can be found on Randal L. Schwartz' home page[1]. As he says:

> One of my latest 'stupid Randal tricks' has been to cruise the net for guest books and see if they accept raw HTML, testing it by feeding it a name or comment of Barney[2]. It is amazing how many of them blindly accept it. (I can't stop giggling when I see the Purple One show up in the list when I reload.)

It is as well to make sure that name fields do not allow the input of HTML, and check whether the home page reference follows the URL syntax. Other checks might involve looking for emtpy fields and rejecting input without a last name or first name.

```
37    # Open guestbook file for writing and lock it.
38    # Check if it exists first.
39    if ( !open (FP, "+<$GUESTFILE") ) {
40        # File not yet there -> create it.
41        open (FP, ">$GUESTFILE")
42            || die "Could not create $GUESTFILE";
43        # Lock file for exclusive access.
44        &lockfile (FP) || die ("Lock failed: $!\n");
45    }
46    else {
47        # Re-open in append mode.
48        open (FP, ">>$GUESTFILE")
49            || die ("Could not append to $GUESTFILE: $!\n");
50        &lockfile (FP) || die ("Lock failed: $!\n");
51    }
52
53    # Append data.
54    if ( length($url) > 0 ){
55        print FP ("<A HREF=\"$url\">$lastname, ",
56                  "$firstname</A><BR>\n");
57    }
58    else {
59        print FP ("$lastname, $firstname<BR>\n");
60    }
61    # Close the file, releasing the lock.
62    close (FP);
63
64    # Create HTML output.
65    print ("<H1> My Virtual Guest Book</H1>\n");
66    print ("<HR>\n");
67    print ("Your data has been entered.\n");
68
69    &html_end ();
70  }
```

---

[1] http://www.teleport.com/~merlyn/
[2] http://www.galcit.caltech.edu/~ta/barney/head.gif

Finally, here is the code to display the guest book forms interface. In order to create a hyperlinked guest list, we simply append the data stored in the guest book file.

```
71  # Display the forms interface.
72  sub send_form {
73
74      local ($scriptname) = $ENV{"SCRIPT_NAME"};
75      print ("<H1>My virtual Guestbook</H1>\n");
76      print ("<FORM $method ACTION=\"$scriptname\">\n");
77
78      print <<"ENDHTML";
79      <P>
80      Please enter your name and home page URL:
81      <P>
82      <INPUT NAME="lastname" SIZE=40> last name <BR>
83      <INPUT NAME="firstname" SIZE=40> first name <BR>
84      <INPUT NAME="url" SIZE=40> home page <BR>
85      <INPUT TYPE="submit" VALUE="Submit..">
86      <HR>
87      These are our virtual guests so far:<P>
88  ENDHTML
89
90      # Now open and display the guestbook. No locking needed.
91      open (FP, "$GUESTFILE");
92      print while <FP>;
93      close (FP);
94      &html_end ();
95  }
```

This mechanism can be used not only for a guest book, but also to report bugs, file complaints, and so on.

7.2.2   Critical regions and semaphores

The period of time for which a program needs exclusive access to shared data is called a *critical region*. In our case, data consistency can only be achieved through *mutual exclusion* of processes in their critical regions. Mutual exclusion can be obtained with a concurrency control mechanism known as *semaphores*, first introduced by Edsger W. Dijkstra [Dijk65]. In its simplest form, a semaphore is an object with two operations, P and V, defined on it (the letters stand for the dutch words 'passeren' and 'vrijgeven', which mean 'pass' and 'release'). The first process to call the P operation continues and can enter its critical region. If another process calls P before the first one has executed the V operation, it blocks and will not continue until the first process has released the semaphore.

A process executing in its critical region has full control over all shared resources, not just over a single file as was the case with the `locking` subroutine defined in Section 5.2.4. However, this file locking technique can be used to implement semaphore functionality since it provides an object (the file) and the P and V operations (locking and releasing).

The following Perl code defines two subroutines, `sema_P` and `sema_V`, that implement a semaphore using file locking.

```
 1  # Semaphore control using a lockfile:
 2  #
 3  #     &sema_P (FH)           # Pass
 4  #     &sema_V (FH)           # Release
 5  #
 6  #     FH is a handle to an opened file, with r/w access.
 7  #
 8  # Return values:
 9  #     1  operation succeeded
10  #     0  failed
11  #
12  # Locking is implemented using the flock(2) system call that is
13  # available on most modern systems.
14  # The sema_P operation will wait if the lockfile is currently
15  # locked by another process.
16  #
17  # Typical use:
18  #
19  #     open (LF, "+>>lockfile") || die (...);
20  #     ...
21  #     if ( &sema_P (LF) ) {
22  #         ...critical region...
23  #     }
24  #     &sema_V (LF);                # release the lock
25
26  sub sema_P {
27      local ($FH) = @_;
28
29      local ($LOCK_EX) = 2;       # lock exclusive
30
31      flock ($FH, $LOCK_EX);       # return TRUE upon success.
32  }
33
34  sub sema_V {
35      local ($FH) = @_;
36
37      local ($LOCK_UN) = 8;       # release the lock
38
39      flock ($FH, $LOCK_UN);       # return TRUE upon success.
40  }
```

7.3   Security issues

One very important aspect of Web transactions is the security of the data transmitted. Since HTTP is a fairly simple and straightforward protocol, it is possible
to create a set-up that allows for eavesdropping on the network for confidential
information. It should be noted that, compared with other operations conducted
via the Internet, the Web does not pose a new or greater security problem. By
logging in to a remote site in order to read email over the Internet, the password
data is transmitted in plain text, and is vulnerable to snooping attacks. However,
since the Web became a popular medium for conducting business at an early stage
in its development, software developers soon began to address the problems of
secure network traffic. Customers are naturally more reluctant to enter details such
as credit card numbers into a fill-out form if the data returned to the server can
potentially be read by a third party. Cryptographic algorithms that provide reasonably secure methods for data transmission and authentication have therefore been
implemented.

There are currently two competing products in existence for providing secure transmission of sensitive data: Terisa Systems' *Secure Hypertext Transfer Protocol* (S-HTTP) and Netscape Communication Corporations *Secure Sockets Layer* (SSL). They both use public key cryptography technology from RSA Data Security Inc. Public key cryptography is a security technique that uses a matched pair of encryption keys. While traditional shared-key cryptography requires correspondents to agree on an encryption key before they can communicate, public key cryptography avoids the need for prior agreement on keys, thus allowing for security provision between mutually unknown parties, a necessary precondition for transactions on the Web.

While Terisa Systems, a joint venture of RSA Inc. and Enterprise Integration Technologies Corp. (EIT), performs encryption on a per-document basis, Netscape's SSL is a fairly low-level transmission protocol that provides a secure transmission channel for higher level application protocols. Protocols such as HTTP and FTP can be layered on top of SSL. Both technologies require specialized Web servers and browsers. While NCSA's Mosaic and its many derivates support S-HTTP, Netscape Navigator uses SSL (however, Netscape Communication Corporations have announced support for both protocols in their product). Both Terisa Systems and Netscape Communication Corporation will be offering software toolkits for developers of Internet applications.

The technology used for the secure transmissions is far from trivial and is really beyond the scope of this book. However, unless you intend to develop client-side software for secure transmissions, the details of encryption and client authentication can be ignored. A gateway application that performs tasks such as evaluating a fill-out form gets its data via the CGI protocol. Providing a secure service does not require any additional programming techniques, as encryption and authentication are handled by the server. The back-end program does not even need to be modified to take advantage of secure transmission features.

Another vital security consideration arises from the fact that client programs transfer information to the server system which is subsequently processed by a gateway program on the server system. The gateway program must ensure that whatever data the client has sent will not violate the system integrity. Shell scripts are traditionally vulnerable to security breaches, since scripts are easy to write and shell programmers are often careless in including checking constraints and errors. Perl provides a facility known as *tainting*, which keeps track of all user data provided to a Perl script and detects when this information is used in situations where it could compromise security, for example in the text of a system command.

7.4   Keeping state information

When writing gateway programs that handle transactions via fill-out forms, problems concerning the need to maintain state information soon arise. Because the

HTTP protocol is stateless the server cannot determine if two accesses from a remote host come from the same user, thus creating an interface that has some kind of memory requires additional programming effort.

A very common example of the need for state information is the virtual shopping cart, as implemented by many commercial sites offering goods and services for sale on the Web. The user browses through a site, and adds items to a shopping cart by selecting links or pressing buttons. Having made several selections, the user can then order the selected articles. Since browsing the electronic store will take the user to many different pages, the shopping cart's contents must somehow be memorized between subsequent accesses.

This section provides a simple example of how state information can be maintained. By analyzing the problems involved in programming the shopping cart mechanism, we discuss techniques for maintaining state information both on the client side and on the server side.

7.4.1   Hidden form fields

Hidden form fields are special 'invisible' elements which are encoded and sent to the server when the form is submitted. The only difference is that unlike a normal forms element, the data does not come from any user input, but is encoded in the HTML document already. Of course, hidden forms fields do not make much sense if the information contained in them is static. It must be generated dynamically on the server side, which is normally done via a gateway program. One very elegant way to do so is to use a template file with special markup embedded in it, and convert this using a string replacement mechanism.

In the following code example, this technique is used to implement a simple shopping cart mechanism for a book store. It works by dynamically generating hidden forms fields which pass state information between multiple user interactions.

Let us first take a look at the HTML template and the output generated from it. Figure 7.2 shows the form as it is initially displayed to the user. It does not look unusual, and except for the multiple submit buttons, there are no visible forms elements. However, parts of this page are generated dynamically. In the HTML code used to display the form, the attributes which describe the book are generated by replacing variables enclosed between dollar signs with the appropriate data.

```
1    <!-- Make sure you edit the ACTION appropriately! -->
2
3    <HEAD>
4    <TITLE> My Virtual Book Store</TITLE>
5    </HEAD>
6    <BODY>
7    <H1> My Virtual Book Store </H1>
8    <HR>
9
10   <FORM METHOD="POST"  ACTION="http://slammer/cgi-neuss/cart1.pl">
11   <H2>Book Order Form</H2>
12   Use the Next and Previous buttons to browse through the
13   list of available books. Use Inspect to look at your shopping
```

My Virtual Book Store

Book Order Form

Use the Next and Previous buttons to browse through the list of available books. Use
Inspect to look at your shopping cart, add a book to the cart with Add, remove it with
Delete.

```
   Author: Larry Wall; Randal Schwartz
    Title: Programming Perl
Publisher: O'Reilley & Associates
     ISBN: 0-937175-64-1

 in cart:
```

Figure 7.2   Shopping cart – initial set-up

My Virtual Book Store

Book Order Form

Use the Next and Previous buttons to browse through the list of available books. Use
Inspect to look at your shopping cart, add a book to the cart with Add, remove it with
Delete.

```
   Author: Larry Wall; Randal Schwartz
    Title: Programming Perl
Publisher: O'Reilley & Associates
     ISBN: 0-937175-64-1

 in cart: yes
```

Figure 7.3   Shopping cart – after adding an item

```
14   cart, add a book to the cart with Add, remove it with Delete.
15
16   <INPUT TYPE="hidden" NAME="item" VALUE="$item$">
17   <INPUT TYPE="hidden" NAME="cart" VALUE="$cart$">
18   <PRE>
19      Author: $auth$
20       Title: $titl$
21   Publisher: $publ$
22        ISBN: $isbn$
23
24    in cart: $isin$
25   </PRE>
26   <input type="submit"  NAME="action"  VALUE="Inspect">
27   <input type="submit"  NAME="action"  VALUE="Add">
28   <input type="submit"  NAME="action"  VALUE="Delete">
29   <input type="submit"  NAME="action"  VALUE="Previous">
30   <input type="submit"  NAME="action"  VALUE="Next">
31   </FORM>
32   <HR>
33   </BODY>
```

These variables serve as placeholders for actual information describing goods available in the virtual store. By selecting the 'Add' button, an item is added to a virtual shopping cart. Figure 7.3 shows the result – the field 'in cart' changes to 'yes' to reflect this fact.

By using the 'Next' and 'Previous' buttons, the user can browse through the inventory. Figure 7.4 shows the contents of the virtual shopping cart as it is displayed when the 'Inspect' button is selected.

Going on to analyze the code that creates these dynamic forms, the first thing needed is a representation for the inventory. This can be simply achieved by defining an associative array, with some unique identifier serving as the key. In the real world, an inventory number or some other internal key would be used for this purpose. Furthermore, a DBM file or even a database system would probably be used rather than an array initialized within the program.

Here is the inventory we use in our example:

```
1   #!/usr/local/bin/perl
2
3   # Location of forms template file.
4   $template = "/igd/a3/home1/neuss/cgi/cart.html";
5
6   # We use a associative array to represent the inventory.
7   %inventory = (
8               'item01',
9                  'Randal Schwartz#Learning Perl#'.
10                 'O\'Reilley & Associates#1-56592-042-2',
11
12              'item02',
13                 'Larry Wall; Randal Schwartz#'.
14                 'Programming Perl#'.
15                 'O\'Reilley & Associates#0-937175-64-1',
16
17              'item03',
18                 'Bruce Webster#Pitfalls of Object-Oriented '.
19                 'Programming#M&T Books#1-55851-397-3'
20             );
```

The code that follows probably looks quite familiar – it decodes the forms input and sets some local variables. When the program is called for the first time, the

---

My Virtual Book Store

Here's your shopping cart:

```
    Author: Randal Schwartz
     Title: Learning Perl
 Publisher: O'Reilley & Associates
      ISBN: 1-56592-042-2

    Author: Bruce Webster
     Title: Pitfalls of Object-Oriented Programming
 Publisher: M&T Books
      ISBN: 1-55851-397-3

    Author: Larry Wall; Randal Schwartz
     Title: Programming Perl
 Publisher: O'Reilley & Associates
      ISBN: 0-937175-64-1
```

Figure 7.4 Shopping cart – inspecting the cart's contents

initial form is sent, along with the first key of our inventory as an argument. The variables item and cart come from the hidden form fields. While item holds the inventory number of the book currently being displayed, cart represents the items selected so far – the contents of the shopping cart. It is encoded as a comma-separated list of item numbers.

```perl
21   # Send HTTP header.
22   &send_header ();
23
24   # Do the real work, trapping any errors.
25   eval { &main; };
26
27   # If an error has occured, log it to STDOUT.
28   if ( $@ ) {
29       &html_start ("Error in Script");
30       print STDOUT ("$@\n");
31       &html_end;
32       exit;
33   }
34
35
36   sub main {
37       # Do we have input?
38       if ( $ENV{'CONTENT_LENGTH'} == 0 &&
39            $ENV{'QUERY_STRING'} eq '' ) {
40
41           # => send first item, empty cart
42           $item = (sort(keys(%inventory)))[0];
43           &send_form ($item, "");
44           return;
45       }
46
47       # Parse forms result and store it in an associative array.
48       %forms = &cgiparse ($request);
49
50       # Fetch some values.
```

```
51        $item = $forms{"item"};
52        $cart = $forms{"cart"};
53        $action = $forms{"action"};
```

After decoding the forms input, the submit buttons are dealt with. In response to an 'Add' or 'Delete' command, the contents of the cart must be modified. This is done by simple string substitution.

```
54        # Handle the "Add" button.
55        if ( $action eq "Add" ) {
56            # If item not yet in cart.
57            unless ( $cart =~ /$item/ ) {
58                $cart .= ($cart eq "") ? $item : ",$item";   # add it
59            }
60        }
61
62        # Handle the "Delete" button.
63        if ( $action eq "Delete" ) {
64            # Delete item from cart.
65            $cart =~ s/$item,?//g;
66            # If item was the last in the list, a ',' remains.
67            $cart =~ s/,$//g;
68        }
```

Code to handle the 'Next' and 'Previous' buttons is also reasonably straightforward. This task consists of finding the next or previous item in the list of inventory keys. Finally, the subroutine send_forms is called to display the subsequent form, except when the 'Inspect' button has been selected, in which case show_cart is called to display the contents of the cart.

```
69        # Handle the "Next" button.
70        if ( $action eq "Next" ) {
71            # Set $item to the successor of $item in @keys.
72            local (@keys) = sort(keys(%inventory));
73            $next = $keys[0];
74            while ( $head = pop (@keys) ) {
75                last if $head eq $item;
76                $next = $head;
77            }
78            $item = $next;
79        }
80
81        # Handle the "Previous" button.
82        if ( $action eq "Previous" ) {
83            # Set $item to the predecessor of $item in @keys.
84            local (@keys) = sort(keys(%inventory));
85            $prev = $keys[@keys-1];
86            while ($tail = shift (@keys) ) {
87                last if $tail eq $item;
88                $prev = $tail;
89            }
90            $item = $prev;
91        }
92
93        # Handle the "Inspect" button.
94        if ( $action eq "Inspect" ) {
95            &show_cart ($cart);
96        }
97
98        if ($action ne "Inspect" ) {
99            &send_form ($item, $cart);
100       }
101
102       &html_end;
103   }
```

The function show_cart creates HTML code to display the shopping cart's contents. It iterates through all the items in the cart. Information from the inventory array is extracted using the current cart element as the key. The value contains four fields separated by '#' characters. These are extracted with the split function.

```
104   # Display the cart contents.
105   sub show_cart {
106       local ($cart) = @_;
107       local (@books) = split (/,/, $cart);
108
109       # Send HTML header.
110       &html_start ("My Virtual Book Store");
111
112       print ("<H1>My Virtual Book Store</H1><HR>\n");
113       print ("<H2>Here's your shopping cart:</H2>\n");
114       print ("<PRE>\n");
115       foreach ( @books ) {
116           &show_book ($_);
117       }
118       print ("</PRE><HR>\n");
119   }
120
121   # Display the details of a given book.
122   sub show_book {
123       local ($item) = @_;
124       ($auth, $titl, $publ, $isbn) = split (/#/, $inventory{$item});
125       print <<"ENDHTML";
126       Author: $auth
127        Title: $titl
128    Publisher: $publ
129         ISBN: $isbn
130
131   ENDHTML
132   }
```

Finally, the forms interface must be generated, and placeholders replaced by the corresponding variable values.

```
133   # Display an item using the forms template.
134   sub send_form {
135       local ($item, $cart) = @_;
136
137       # Is the given item already in the cart?
138       local ($isin) = ($cart =~ /$item/) ? "yes" : "-";
139
140       # Open form template file.
141       open (FP, "$template") || die ("$template: $!\n");
142
143       ($auth, $titl, $publ, $isbn) = split (/#/,$inventory{$item});
144
145       # Copy while replacing embedded variables.
146       while ( <FP> ) {
147           s/\$item\$/$item/g;
148           s/\$cart\$/$cart/g;
149           s/\$auth\$/$auth/g;
150           s/\$titl\$/$titl/g;
151           s/\$publ\$/$publ/g;
152           s/\$isbn\$/$isbn/g;
153           s/\$isin\$/$isin/g;
154           print;
155       }
156       close(FP);
157   }
```

As is apparent, hidden form fields are quite easy to use, and provide a simple and effective mechanism for passing state information between forms. Unfortunately they have one major drawback, which limits their use to simple applications. Since state information is kept on the client side within the current document, whenever the browser's 'Back to Previous Document' function is used, all state information gathered in the last step is lost. For more sophisticated applications, state information must be kept on the server side. The next section discusses another version of the shopping cart program, which stores state information on the server side.

7.4.2   State information on the server side

While hidden form fields provide a simple and elegant way of maintaining state information across forms interactions, there are situations when this approach is inadequate. Developing the 'book store' example from the previous section illustrates typical problems that arise. The addition of a search facility enables book details to be traced by entering the author's name or the book title in a fill-out form. The following HTML code produces a simple fill-out form for this task.

```
 1  <HEAD>
 2  <TITLE> My Virtual Book Store</TITLE>
 3  </HEAD>
 4  <BODY>
 5  <H1> My Virtual Book Store </H1>
 6  <HR>
 7
 8  <FORM METHOD="POST"
 9   ACTION="http://slammer/cgi-neuss/cart2.pl">
10  <H2>Book Search Form</H2>
11  Search by Author, Title, Publisher, or ISBN. Enter the author's
12  name in the form <I>Lastname, Firstname</I>. Searches are
13  case-insensitive.
14
15  <PRE>
16     <B>Author</B>:  <INPUT NAME="auth" SIZE=20>
17      <B>Title</B>:  <INPUT NAME="titl" SIZE=20>
18  <B>Publisher</B>:  <INPUT NAME="publ" SIZE=20>
19       <B>ISBN</B>:  <INPUT NAME="isbn" SIZE=20>
20
21  </PRE>
22  <input type="submit"  NAME="action"  VALUE="Search">
23  </FORM>
24  <HR>
25  </BODY>
```

Figure 7.5 shows how the form is rendered by a browser. Entering an author name and selecting the 'Search' button calls up a gateway program which produces the output shown in Figure 7.6. The list of books matching the query is displayed as hyperlinks leading to the virtual book order page familiar from the previous section.

Since this form is generated by a gateway program, key information can simply be encoded into the hyperlink for each item so that the link leads to the page for the book.

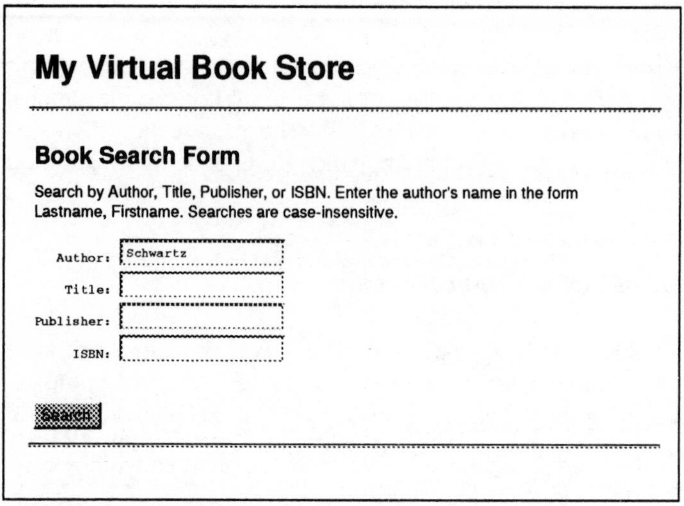

Figure 7.5   Shopping cart – search interface

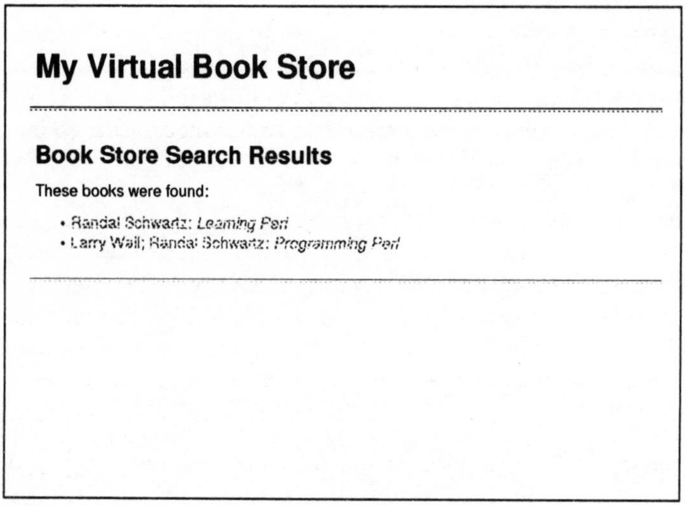

Figure 7.6   Shopping cart – search result

For example:

```
 1  <HEAD>
 2  <TITLE> My Virtual Book Store</TITLE>
 3  </HEAD>
 4  <BODY>
 5  <H1> My Virtual Book Store</H1>
 6  <HR>
 7  <H2> Book Store Search Results </H2>
 8  These books were found:
 9  <UL>
10  <LI> <A HREF="/cgi-neuss/cart2.pl?item=item01">
11  Randal Schwartz: <I>Learning Perl</I>
12  </A><BR>
13  <LI> <A HREF="/cgi-neuss/cart2.pl?item=item02">
14  Larry Wall; Randal Schwartz: <I>Programming perl</I>
15  </A><BR>
16  </UL>
17  <HR>
18  </BODY></HTML>
```

By selecting a hyperlink, the gateway program is called with the arguments 'item=item01', exactly as if they had been entered in a forms field. It can then display a page with the corresponding book information as already shown in Figure 7.2. Problems are almost inevitable after the user selects 'Add' to enter a book into the virtual shopping cart. The most likely course of action would be for the user to select the browser's 'Back' button to return to the page displaying the search results. Then, by selecting a different link, the user might inspect another book, only to find that all of a sudden their shopping cart was empty.

What has happened is as follows. The shopping cart uses hidden form fields to hold state information. Since this information is stored inside the document, it will only be passed back to the server when a form submission from that document is made. However, if another navigation method such as the browser's 'Back' button is used, the client jumps from the document containing the hidden fields to a document previously visited. Of course, this earlier document does not contain the values of hidden fields in the later form, and thus any changes made to the shopping cart contents are lost.

In short, navigating through documents via the Browser's 'Back' button or history list destroys state information stored in hidden fields. In a situation where a user is likely to use these navigational features, state information, such the contents of the shopping cart, must be stored on the server side. One possible solution is to squirrel away information in a file on the server side, and use a simple naming scheme to create a unique identifier that maps to this file. By passing this identifier back to the client (and encoding it into every URL that is generated dynamically so that it doesn't get lost), the server hands the client a 'key' with which it can access and modify the server state. This key remains constant throughout the complete transaction, and thus jumps through the browser's history list do not cause any information loss. Transactions with server side state are more difficult to implement, and require that a way is found to 'clean up' if a key is not used for a specific period of time, otherwise, the disk will gradually fill up with unfinished client transactions.

In this section, a very simple mechanism is used to provide server side state information. Using the file locking technique from Section 7.2, the code increments a simple counter on every occasion that a new connection to the search page is made. This counter then serves as a transaction identifier, which uniquely identifies a sequence of interactions by the same client. The transaction identifier is used to create a naming scheme for server side files, and the shopping cart information is stored in that file.

We start by defining the file locations for the shopping cart files and a common file which holds the counter.

```
1    #!/usr/local/bin/perl
2
3    # Location of "Search" forms template file.
4    $SEARCH="/Users/neuss/cgi/cart2sea.htm";
5
6    # Location of "Book" forms template file.
7    $BOOK="/Users/neuss/cgi/cart2boo.htm";
8
9    # Location of the counter file.
10   $COUNTFILE="/Users/neuss/tmp/COUNT";
11
12   # Location of the cart file directory.
13   $CARTDIR="/Users/neuss/tmp";
14
15   %inventory = (
16               'item01',
17               'Randal Schwartz#Learning Perl#'.
18               'O\'Reilley & Associates#1-56592-042-2',
19
20               'item02',
21               'Larry Wall; Randal Schwartz#'.
22               'Programming Perl#'.
23               'O\'Reilley & Associates#0-937175-64-1',
24
25               'item03',
26               'Bruce Webster#Pitfalls of Object-Oriented '.
27               'Programming#M&T Books#1-55851-397-3'
28   );
29
30   # Output the HTTP header.
31   &send_header ();
32
33   # Do the real work, trapping any errors.
34   eval { &main; };
35
36   # If an error has occured, log it to STDOUT.
37   if ( $@ ) {
38       &html_start ("Error in Script");
39       print STDOUT ("$@\n");
40       &html_end;
41       exit;
42   }
```

When the first call to the search form is made, a unique identifier is generated by incrementing a counter and prefixing it with the constant string 'ID'. The function write_cart is called up with an empty cart string in order to create a new shopping cart file, then the search form is generated, with a hidden forms variable id replaced by the identifier string that has just been generated.

```
43   sub main {
44
45       # Send HTML header.
```

```
46        &html_start ("My Virtual Book Store");
47
48        # Do we have input?
49        if ( $ENV{'CONTENT_LENGTH'} == 0 &&
50            $ENV{'QUERY_STRING'} eq '' ) {
51
52            # No - this is the first call: create the id
53            $id = "ID" . &uniqcount ($COUNTFILE);
54
55            # Create an empty cart file.
56            & write_cart ($id, "");
57
58            # Send the "Search" form template.
59            &send_searchform ($id);
60
61            return;
62        }
63
64        # Parse forms result and store it in an associative array.
65        %forms = &cgiparse ($request);
66
67        # Fetch some values.
68        $item = $forms{"item"};
69        $action = $forms{"action"};
70        $id = $forms{"id"};
```

To perform the search each inventory item in turn is compared with the expressions entered in the search fields. If a match is found, a hyperlink is constructed which has name–value pairs for id and item appended to the script path.

```
71        # If we come from the "Search" form
72        # perform search by comparing against the inventory.
73        if ( $action eq "Search" ) {
74            $auth = $forms{"auth"};
75            $titl = $forms{"titl"};
76            $publ = $forms{"publ"};
77            $isbn = $forms{"isbn"};
78
79            foreach ( sort(keys(%inventory)) ) {
80                ($au, $ti, $pu, $is) = split (/#/, $inventory{$_});
81                # If book matches query...
82                if ( ($au =~ /.?$auth/i)  &&
83                     ($ti =~ /.?$titl/i)  &&
84                     ($pu =~ /.?$publ/i)  &&
85                     ($is =~ /.?$isbn/i) ) {
86                    # ..create a dynamic hyperlink to it.
87                    $hits .= "<LI> <A HREF=\"$ENV{SCRIPT_NAME}";
88                    $hits .= "?id=$id&item=$_\">\n";
89                    $hits .= "$au: <I>$ti</I></A><BR>\n";
90                }
91            }
```

Next, the HTML code for the list of matches is generated. After returning it to the client, the HTTP trailer is sent, and the program terminates.

```
92            # Create output.
93            print ("<H1> My Virtual Book Store</H1>\n");
94            print ("<HR>\n");
95            print ("<H2> Book Store Search Results </H2>\n");
96
97            # If there are books matching the query.
98            if ( length($hits) > 0 ) {
99                print ("These books were found:\n");
100               print ("<UL>\n$hits\n</UL>\n");
101           }
102           else {
103               print ("No books match your query.\n");
```

```
104        }
105        print ("<HR>\n");
106
107        # Send HTTP trailer and return.
108        &html_end;
109        return;
110    }
```

The 'Add' and 'Delete' buttons are handled in essentially the same way as in the previous shopping cart example. The only difference is that instead of generating a hidden form field to store the cart contents, the cart file identified by id is used. After adding or deleting an item, a short message is generated. By not providing any hyperlink in the acknowledgment message, the user is compelled to navigate back to the search result page by means of the browser's 'Back' button.

An interaction sequence such as that described here relies strongly on navigation backwards to dynamically generated pages. The page containing the search results is usually visited several times, each time the user follows another link which originates in it. Thus care should be taken to provide as simple an interaction as possible in the pages that follow – every additional hyperlink the user follows adds to the browsers history, and makes it more difficult to return to the search result page.

```
111        # Otherwise, we've been called from the "Book" form.
112        # Handle the "Add", "Delete", or "Inspect" buttons.
113
114        # Get the cart info from file.
115        $cart = &read_cart ($id);
116
117        # Handle the "Add" button.
118        if ( $action eq "Add" ) {
119            # If item not yet in cart.
120            unless ( $cart =~ /$item/ ) {
121                $cart .= ($cart eq "") ? $item : ",$item";   # add it
122            }
123            # Write modified cart to file.
124            &write_cart ($id, $cart);
125
126            # Acknowledge with a short message.
127            print ("<H1>Added to Cart</H1>\n");
128            print ("<HR>\n");
129            print ("Book added to cart.\n");
130            &html_end;
131            return;
132        }
133
134        # Handle the "Delete" button.
135        if ( $action eq "Delete" ) {
136            # Delete item from cart.
137            $cart =~ s/$item,?//g;
138            # If item was the last in the list, a ',' remains.
139            $cart =~ s/,$//g;
140            # Write modified cart to file.
141            &write_cart ($id, $cart);
142
143            # Acknowledge with a short message.
144            print ("<H1>Delete from Cart</H1>\n");
145            print ("<HR>\n");
146            print ("Book deleted from cart.\n");
147            &html_end;
148            return;
149        }
```

Handling the 'Inspect' button is straightforward – the cart contents are read from the file and displayed.

```
150     # Handle the "Inspect" button.
151     if ( $action eq "Inspect" ) {
152         # Display the shopping cart.
153         &show_cart ($cart);
154         &html_end;
155         return;
156     }
157
158     # Send new book form template.
159     &send_bookform ($item, $cart);
160
161     &html_end;
162 }
```

Here is the code that reads and writes the cart files. Since we have already made sure that every customer gets a unique transaction identifier, there is no need to bother with concurrency and file locking.

```
163 # Write cart file.
164 sub write_cart {
165     local ($id, $cart) = @_;
166     open (FPOUT, ">$CARTDIR/cart$id") ||
167         die ("$CARTDIR/cart$id: $!\n");
168     print FPOUT ($cart);
169     close(FPOUT);
170 }
171
172 # Read cart file.
173 sub read_cart {
174     local ($id) = @_;
175     open (FPIN, "$CARTDIR/cart$id") ||
176         die("$CARTDIR/cart$id: $!\n");
177     $cart = <FPIN>;
178     close (FPIN);
179     $cart;
180 }
```

The function uniqcount increments a counter every time it is accessed and uses file locking as described in Section 5.2.4. The counter value can be used to generate unique identifiers. If you want to use a more sophisticated scheme which generates transaction identifiers, which are less easily predictable, you could use a simple hash function, or append a random string to each identifier.

```
181 # uniqcount - create unique identifier.
182 sub uniqcount {
183     local ($lockfile) = @_;
184     if ( !open (COUNT, "+<$lockfile")){
185         # File not yet there -> create it.
186         open (COUNT, "+>$lockfile")
187             || die ("Could not create $lockfile");
188         # Lock file for exclusive access.
189         &lockfile (COUNT) || die ("Couldn't lock: $!\n");
190         print COUNT ("0\n");
191         $count = 0;
192     }
193     else {
194         &lockfile (COUNT) || die ("Couldn't lock: $!\n");
195         $count = <COUNT>;
196     }
197
198     # Update with an incremented value.
199     seek (COUNT, 0, 0); # rewind
```

```
200        $count++;
201        print COUNT ("$count\n");
202
203        # Close the file, releasing the lock.
204        close (COUNT);
205
206        # Return value.
207        $count;
208    }
```

The functions send_bookform, send_searchform, show_cart, and show_book are essentially identical to their equivalent from the previous section, and are therefore not listed here.

Appendix A

Commented Listings

This appendix contains a number of useful programs that illustrate the material discussed in this book. Some of them may be used without alteration, others may need to be tailored to your particular system before they will work.

The sample programs are all derived from real life programs and have been adapted to conform to the conventions used through this book. However, at some places you may notice that the sample programs violate our own guidelines. This is intended to prevent you from thoughtlessly copying something that someone else has written. Always make sure you know what you are doing – it is *your* computer and *your* information!

A.1   Electronic registration

Fill-out forms provide the most obvious way of gathering user data for any kind of transaction. Using forms elements, an electronic order form can be placed right next to the product or service a Web page is advertising. The recent development of secure HTTP transaction mechanisms allows sensitive information such as credit card numbers to be transmitted with a reasonable level of security.

This section uses electronic conference registration as an example to introduce and discuss the elements of a complex interactive transaction conducted via forms. The code was developed to handle the conference registration for the Third International World Wide Web Conference in April 1995 and later adapted for the Federal Webmaster Conference registration by Kim Stephenson of NCSA.

The electronic registration program is a rather complex example which uses the techniques introduced in Section 6.4.2 to save state information across multiple client calls. Maintaining client state information is necessary to provide users with the possibility of reviewing their data before finally confirming the registration.

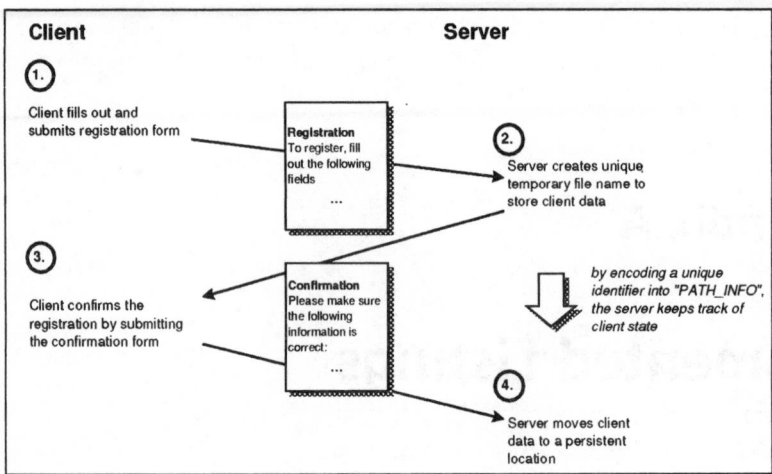

Figure A.1   Electronic registration: flow of data

Figure A.1 shows how information flows between server and client.

The gateway program takes care of various things, including concurrency control, and a stateful transaction (Section 6.4.2), which is implemented by encoding a 'magic cookie'[1] into the URL path). The program works as follows:

- The client fills out a form and submits it. The gateway program checks for validity of data and sends back an error message if an entry is missing or obviously inconsistent. If the input data is found to be correct, the program generates a unique 'cookie' string (function `makecookie`). Using a lock-file mechanism (Section 5.2.4) ensures that the cookie string is unique, even when clients access the registration program simultaneously.

- Using the cookie string to create file names, the client data is written to the local file system, and confirmation is sent to the client. By appending the cookie to the script path, the transaction identifier is transmitted back to the server when the user selects 'Send Registration' from the confirmation page.

- After the user has confirmed the registration, the function `confirmregis` is called. The gateway program can distinguish between the registration and the confirmation phases by looking at the `PATH_INFO` variable. If the user has confirmed registration, the cookie string is extracted from `PATH_INFO` and used to construct the file names.

- Finally, the program moves the registration data from the temporary directory `DUMP_DIR` to its ultimate destination, and sends an email message as confirmation.

---

[1] Using a cookie string to provide state and construct file names is a technique initially introduced by Ari Luotonen in his registration programs for WWW94 held at CERN. For the WWW95 registration, I adopted this concept but added a locking mechanism to handle concurrency – C.N.

Section A.1.2 lists the HTML code which creates the forms interface, Section A.1.3 contains the Perl code which handles the gateway program, creates a confirmation page, and stores the data to file system files.

A.1.1   Registration form

Figure A.2   Federal Webmaster Workshop registration form

Figure A.2 shows the registration form as it appears when loaded by a Web browser. Since we use the registration form for demonstration purposes only, it has been significantly edited and shortened. The next section lists the HTML code used to create the form. Section A.1.3 lists the code which evaluates the query data submitted by the client.

A.1.2 Listing: `reg-form.html`

This section contains the HTML code that generates the fill-out form for the electronic registration.

```
1   <HEAD>
2   <TITLE>1995 Federal Webmasters Workshop Registration Form</TITLE>
3   </HEAD>
4
5   <BODY>
6   <H2>Federal Webmasters Workshop July 11-13, 1995.</h2>
7   <I>This is an abbreviated and edited version of the registration
8   form used for the Federal Webmasters Workshop
9   July 11-13, 1995.</I>
10  <HR>
11
12  <FORM METHOD=GET ACTION="http://slammer/cgi-bin/eval-reg.pl">
13  <H3>Personal Information</H3>
14    <INPUT TYPE="text" SIZE="40" NAME="Lname">
15      Last Name<BR>
16    <INPUT TYPE="text" SIZE="40" NAME="Fname">
17     First Name
18    <INPUT TYPE="text" SIZE="1" NAME="Init">
19     Middle Initial<BR>
20    <INPUT TYPE="text" SIZE="20" NAME="agency">
21     Federal Agency - Please use acronym, e.g. NIH<BR>
22    <INPUT TYPE="text" SIZE="20" NAME="email">
23     email address<BR>
24  <HR>
25
26  <H3>Payment Information</H3>
27  <B>Please check one of these items:</B>
28  <DL>
29
30  <DD><INPUT TYPE="radio"  NAME="pay" value="k">Check <BR>
31  Make payable to Encore Management Corporation,<BR>
32  1140 Connecticut Ave. N. W., Suite 501, Washington,
33  D. C. 20036<P>
34  <DD><INPUT TYPE="radio"  NAME="pay" value="c">
35     Credit card (Master Card,
36     VISA, and American Express) <BR>
37         Note: If are paying by credit card  please call
38         to leave your credit card information.<P>
39  <DD><INPUT TYPE="radio"  NAME="pay" value="p" >
40     Gov't Purchase or Training
41     Order (Enter number below).<BR>
42         Please provide PO number by 20 June, 1995<BR>
43  <INPUT TYPE="text" SIZE="50" NAME="ponum"><P>
44  </DL>
45  <HR>
46  <H3>Attendance Information:</H3>
47
48  <B>  Check each session you plan to attend:</B>
49  <DL>
50  <DD><INPUT TYPE="checkbox" NAME="day1" VALUE="Y">
51     First day sessions on Tues, July 11
52  <DD><INPUT TYPE="checkbox" NAME="day2" VALUE="Y">
53     Second day sessions on Wednesday, July 12
54  <DD><INPUT TYPE="checkbox" NAME="day3" VALUE="Y">
55     Informal sessions on Thursday, July 13
56     (no meal sessions)<BR>
57  </DL>
58
59  <B>There will be two different tracks for the second day
60     sessions:<BR>
61         Please indicate your level of interest.</B><P>
62  <DL>
63  <DD><INPUT TYPE="radio" NAME="level1" VALUE="Expert">
```

```
64              Expert Track
65              (Some experience already in providing Web services)
66  <DD><INPUT TYPE="radio" NAME="level1" VALUE="Novice" CHECKED>
67              Novice Track
68              (New to the area, or planning to provide services
69               in the future)
70  </DL>
71
72  <INPUT TYPE="submit" VALUE=" Send Registration ">
73
74  </FORM>
75  </BODY>
```

A.1.3   Listing: `eval-reg.pl`

Here is the Perl code for the registration gateway program. It checks input data validity, creates registration numbers, and maintains a stateful transaction in order to provide users with an automatic confirmation form.

Upon successful confirmation, an email message is automatically sent to the user.

```perl
1   #!/usr/local/bin/perl
2
3   # CGI/1.0 script to handle WWW95 Conference
4   # tutorial/workshop registration.
5   #
6   # Modified by: Kim Stephenson (NCSA) 03/28/95
7   # Re-edited for use in "Webmasters Handbook" by Christian Neuss
8   # and Johan Vromans.
9
10  # Some global settings
11  umask(002);
12
13  $WEBMASTER = "itfc\@ncsa.uiuc.edu";
14  $COOKIEFILE = "/var/webmaster/regfiles/COOKIE";
15  $COUNTFILE = "/var/webmaster/regfiles/COUNT";
16
17  $METADIR = "/var/webmaster/regfiles/META";
18  $DUMPDIR = "/var/webmaster/regfiles/DUMP";
19  $SPOOLDIR = "/var/webmaster/regfiles/INCOMING";
20
21  # This program does not use the sendmail routine from the book.
22  # Make sure you have the correct path for sendmail:
23  $SENDMAIL = "/usr/lib/sendmail";
24
25  # Send the HTTP header.
26  &send_header ();
27
28  # Do the real work, trapping any errors.
29  eval { &main; };
30
31  # If an error has occured, log it to STDOUT.
32  if ( $@ ) {
33      &html_start ("Federal Webmaster Conference registration");
34      print STDOUT ("$@\n");
35      &html_end;
36  }
37
38  # The main work.
39  sub main {
40
41      # Check for a coockie. If we have one, confirm...
42      if ( length($ENV{"PATH_INFO"}) > 0 ) {
43          &confirmregis ();
44      }
```

```
45      else {
46          # ... otherwise register.
47          &parseregis ();
48      }
49  }
50
51  sub parseregis {
52      local ($err);
53      &html_start ("Federal Webmaster Conference registration");
54
55      # Get CGI data.
56      %form = &cgiparse ();
57      $form{"arrive"}  =~ s/[^0-9]*([0-9]*)/\1/;
58      $form{"depart"}  =~ s/[^0-9]*([0-9]*)/\1/;
59
60      # Get rid of characters we don't want in here.
61      foreach $w ( sort(keys(%form)) ) {
62          $form{$w} =~ tr/\n\r\t^/ /s;
63      }
64
65      # Check for validity.
66      unless ( length($form{"Lname"}) > 0
67              && length($form{"Fname"}) > 0 ) {
68          $err .= "<LI>We need first- and last name!\n";
69      }
70      unless ( length($form{"agency"}) > 0 ) {
71          $err .= "<LI>Please provide your agency\n";
72      }
73
74      # Issue error messages, if any.
75      if ( $err ) {
76          print ("<H1>Error - Some Fields Missing</H1>");
77          print ("You need to supply the following information\n");
78          print ("before your registration can be processed:\n");
79          print ("<UL>\n");
80          print ($err);
81          print ("</UL>\n");
82          &html_end;
83          return;
84      }
85
86      # It appears valid, make coockie.
87      $COOKIE = &makecookie ($COOKIEFILE);
88      $SPOOLFILE = "$SPOOLDIR/$COOKIE.meta";
89
90      unless ( open (FP, ">$SPOOLFILE") ) {
91          print ("Couldn't open spool $SPOOLFILE: $!\n");
92          die ("Couldn't open spool $SPOOLFILE: $!");
93      }
94      &savedata (*FP);
95      close (FP);
96
97      # Generate a form to confirm this registry.
98      $script = $ENV{"SCRIPT_NAME"};
99      print <<"ENDHTML";
100     <H1>Confirmation</H1>
101     <B>Make sure</B> that the following information is correct,
102     and then press the <B>Send Registration</B> button.
103     If there is an error, go back to registration form page,
104     correct errors, and re-send it (and forget this page).<P>
105     <FORM ACTION="${script}/${COOKIE}">
106     <INPUT TYPE="submit" VALUE="Send Registration">
107     </FORM><P>
108     <HR>
109 ENDHTML
110     print ("<PRE>\n");
111     &printdata (*STDOUT);
112     print ("</PRE>\n");
113     &html_end;
```

```perl
114  }
115
116  sub confirmregis {
117
118      &html_start ("Federal Webmaster Conference ".
119                   "Registration Confirmation");
120
121      # Get cookie from PATH_INFO, various inits:
122      $PATH_INFO = $ENV{"PATH_INFO"};
123      ($COOKIE = $PATH_INFO) =~ s/\/(.*)/$1/;
124
125      if ( length("$COOKIE") == 0 ) {
126          print ("<H1>Error: No magic cookie</H1>");
127          &html_end;
128          exit (0);
129      }
130
131      $SPOOLFILE = "$SPOOLDIR/$COOKIE.meta";
132
133      unless ( -f "$SPOOLFILE" ) {
134          print <<EOD;
135  <H1>Error: Invalid magic cookie ($COOKIE)</H1>
136  The cookie is either corrupt, expired or already used.<P>
137  <I>(You have probably already confirmed)</I><P>
138  <ADDRESS>$WEBMASTER</ADDRESS>
139  EOD
140          &html_end;
141          exit (0);
142      }
143
144      $count = &uniqcount ($COUNTFILE);
145      $REGNUM = "V$count";
146      $METAFILE = "$METADIR/V$count-$COOKIE.meta";
147      $DUMPFILE = "$DUMPDIR/V$count-$COOKIE.dmp";
148
149      unless (rename ($SPOOLFILE, $METAFILE) ) {
150          print ("<P><B>couldn't rename(): $!</B>\n");
151          print ("<P>From: $SPOOLFILE\n");
152          print ("<P>To: $METAFILE\n");
153          die ("couldnt rename() $!\n");
154      }
155      unless (open (FPIN, "<$METAFILE") ) {
156          print ("<P><B>couldn't open(): $!</B>\n");
157          print ("<P>File: $METAFILE\n");
158          die ("couldn't open(): $!\n");
159      }
160      unless (open (FPOUT, ">$DUMPFILE") ) {
161          print ("<P><B>couldn't open(): $!</B>\n");
162          print ("<P>File: $DUMPFILE\n");
163          die ("couldn't open(): $!\n");
164      }
165      while ( <FPIN> ) {
166          if ( m/\s*(\S*)\s*:\s*(.*)/ ) {
167              $form{$1} = $2;
168              print FPOUT ("^$2^,");
169          }
170      }
171      print FPOUT ("\n");
172      close (FPIN);
173      close (FPOUT);
174
175      # Registration completed.
176      print ("<H1>Registration complete</H1>\n");
177      print ("Your registration number is $REGNUM.\n");
178      print ("This is the data which has been assigned:\n");
179      print ("<PRE>\n");
180      &printdata (*STDOUT);
181      print ("</PRE>\n");
182      &html_end;
```

```
183
184         # Send mail.
185         local ($mailto) = $form{"email"};
186         if ( length($mailto) > 0 ) {
187         unless ( open (FPM,
188                        "| $SENDMAIL -f $WEBMASTER $mailto".
189                        ">/dev/null 2>&1" ) ) {
190             print ("<P><B>couldn't open pipe to sendmail: $!</B>\n");
191             die ("couldn't open pipe to sendmail: $!\n");
192         }
193
194         &mailuser (*FPM);
195         close (FPM);
196
197         print ("<P>\n");
198         print ("An automatic email message has been sent to you\n");
199         print ("about this.\n");
200     }
201 }
202
203 # mailuser -- mail the confirmation to the user.
204 sub mailuser {
205     local (*FP2) = @_;
206     print FP2 <<EOD;
207 Subject: Registration $REGNUM of $form{"Lname"}
208
209 You have been assigned the registration number $REGNUM.
210 Please refer to this number in future communications
211 with the conference committee.
212
213 You can get up to date information on the registration
214 process by accessing:
215   http://skydive.ncsa.uiuc.edu/webmast-reg/registration.html
216
217 Here's the info we're putting into the database:
218
219 EOD
220     &maildata (*FP2);
221
222     print FP2 <<EOD;
223
224 ----------------------------------------------------
225 (Mail automatically sent by a script - do not reply)
226 EOD
227 }
228
229 # Store the registration data.
230 # This subroutine and the others following it are a splendid
231 # example of not using subroutines and formats. -- jv
232 sub savedata {
233     local (*FP) = @_;
234     $Lname = $form{"Lname"};
235     $Mname = $form{"Init"};
236     $Fname = $form{"Fname"};
237     $Agency = $form{"agency"};
238     $email = $form{"email"};
239     $pay = $form{"pay"};
240     $ponum = $form{"ponumber"};
241     $day1 = $form{"day1"};
242     $day2 = $form{"day2"};
243     $level1 = $form{"level1"};
244
245     printf FP ("%-10s %s\n", "Lname:", $Lname);
246     printf FP ("%-10s %s\n", "Fname:", $Fname);
247     printf FP ("%-10s %s\n", "Init:", $Mname);
248     printf FP ("%-10s %s\n", "agency:", $Agency);
249     printf FP ("%-10s %s\n", "email:", $email);
250     printf FP ("%-10s %s\n", "pay:", $pay);
251     printf FP ("%-10s %s\n", "ponumber: ", $ponum);
```

```
252         printf FP ("%-10s %s\n", "day1: ", $day1);
253         printf FP ("%-10s %s\n", "day2: ", $day2);
254         printf FP ("%-10s %s\n", "level1: ", $level1);
255    }
256
257    sub printdata {
258        local (*FP) = @_;
259        $Lname = $form{"Lname"};
260        $Mname = $form{"Init"};
261        $Fname = $form{"Fname"};
262        $Agency = $form{"agency"};
263        $email = $form{"email"};
264        $pay = $form{"pay"};
265        $ponum = $form{"ponumber"};
266        $day1 = $form{"day1"};
267        $day2 = $form{"day2"};
268        $level1 = $form{"level1"};
269
270        printf FP ("%-10s\n", "<H2>Personal Information</h2>");
271        printf FP ("%-10s %s\n",
272                    "Last Name:                    ", $Lname);
273        printf FP ("%-10s %s\n",
274                    "First Name:                   ", $Fname);
275        printf FP ("%-10s %s\n",
276                    "Middle Initial:               ", $Mname);
277        printf FP ("%-10s %s\n",
278                    "Federal Agency:               ", $Agency);
279        printf FP ("%-10s %s\n",
280                    "email:                        ", $email);
281
282        printf FP ("%-10s\n", "<HR>");
283        printf FP ("%-10s\n", "<H2>Payment Information</h2>");
284        if ( $pay eq "p" ) {
285            printf FP ("%-10s\n",
286                        "Pay By:                   Purchase Order");
287        }
288        elsif ( $pay eq "k" ) {
289            printf FP ("%-10s\n",
290                        "Pay By:                   Check");
291        }
292        else {
293            printf FP ("%-10s\n",
294                        "Pay By:                   Credit");
295        }
296        printf FP ("%-10s %s\n",
297                    "Purchase Order Number:     ", $ponum);
298
299        printf FP ("%-10s\n", "<HR>");
300        printf FP ("%-10s\n", "<H2>Attendance Information</h2>");
301        if ( $day1 ) {
302            printf FP ("%-10s \n",
303                        "First Day:                YES");
304        }
305        else {
306            printf FP ("%-10s \n",
307                        "First Day:                NO");
308        }
309        if ( $day2 ) {
310            printf FP ("%-10s \n",
311                        "Second Day:               YES");
312        }
313        else {
314            printf FP ("%-10s \n",
315                        "Second Day:               NO");
316        }
317        if ( $level1 eq "Expert" ) {
318            printf FP ("%-10s \n", "Experienced Track");
319        }
320        else {
```

```
321             printf FP ("%-10s \n", "Novice Track");
322         }
323     }
324
325     sub maildata {
326         local (*FP) = @_;
327         $Lname = $form{"Lname"};
328         $Mname = $form{"Init"};
329         $Fname = $form{"Fname"};
330         $Agency = $form{"agency"};
331         $email = $form{"email"};
332         $pay = $form{"pay"};
333         $ponum = $form{"ponumber"};
334         $day1 = $form{"day1"};
335         $day2 = $form{"day2"};
336         $level1 = $form{"level1"};
337
338         printf FP ("%-10s\n", "-"x52);
339         printf FP ("%-10s\n", "Personal Information");
340         printf FP ("%-10s\n", "-"x52);
341         printf FP ("%-10s %s\n", "Last Name:        ", $Lname);
342         printf FP ("%-10s %s\n", "First Name:       ", $Fname);
343         printf FP ("%-10s %s\n", "Middle Initial: ", $Mname);
344         printf FP ("%-10s %s\n", "Federal Agency: ", $Agency);
345         printf FP ("%-10s %s\n", "email:            ", $email);
346
347         printf FP ("%-10s\n", "-"x52);
348         printf FP ("%-10s\n", "Payment Information");
349         printf FP ("%-10s\n", "-"x52);
350         if ( $pay eq "p" ) {
351             printf FP ("%-10s\n", "Pay By: Purchase Order");
352         }
353         elsif ( $pay eq "k" ) {
354             printf FP ("%-10s\n", "Pay By: Check");
355         }
356         else {
357             printf FP ("%-10s\n", "Pay By: Credit");
358         }
359         printf FP ("%-10s %s\n", "Purchase Order Number: ", $ponum);
360
361         printf FP ("%-10s\n", "-"x52);
362         printf FP ("%-10s\n", "Attendance Information");
363         printf FP ("%-10s\n", "-"x52);
364         if ( $day1 ) {
365             printf FP ("%-10s \n", "First Day: YES");
366         }
367         else {
368             printf FP ("%-10s \n", "First Day: NO");
369         }
370         if ( $day2 ) {
371             printf FP ("%-10s \n", "Second Day: YES");
372         }
373         else {
374             printf FP ("%-10s \n", "Second Day: NO");
375         }
376         if ( $level1 eq "Expert" ) {
377             printf FP ("%-10s \n", "Experienced Track");
378         }
379         else {
380             printf FP ("%-10s \n", "Novice Track");
381         }
382     }
383
384     # makecookie - create magic cookie
385     sub makecookie {
386         local ($cookiefile) = @_;
387         $now = &getdate ();
388         $count = &uniqcount ($cookiefile);
389         "T$count-$now";
```

```
390    }
391
392    # getdate - ou est le neige d'hier?
393    sub getdate {
394        local ($sec,$min,$hour,$mday,$mon,$year,
395               $wday,@dontcare)= localtime (time);
396        local ($now) =
397            sprintf ("%2.2d.%2.2d.%2.2d-%2.2d:%2.2d:%2.2d",
398                     $mday,$mon+1,$year,$hour,$min,$sec);
399        $now;
400    }
401
402    # uniqcount - create unique identifier
403    sub uniqcount {
404        local ($lockfile) = @_;
405        if ( !open (COUNT, "+<$lockfile") ) {
406            # File not yet there -> create it.
407            open (COUNT, "+>$lockfile") ||
408                die ("Could not create $lockfile: $!\n");
409            # Lock file for exclusive access.
410            &lockfile (COUNT) || die ("Couldn't lock: $!\n");
411            print COUNT ("0\n");
412            $count = 0;
413        }
414        else {
415            &lockfile (COUNT) || die ("Could not lock: $!\n");
416            $count = <COUNT>;
417        }
418
419        # Update the count value.
420        seek (COUNT,0,0); # rewind
421        $count++;
422        print COUNT ("$count\n");
423
424        # Close file, releasing the lock.
425        close(COUNT);
426
427        $count; # return value
428    }
```

A.2   Log analysis

A.2.1   Listing: `errlog.pl`

This section contains the complete code of the error log file reporting utility from Section 6.2.2. We have added code that creates an email message and sends it to the owner of the file that caused the error. By counting the outgoing mail messages per user, we make sure that a maximum number of automatic mailings is not exceeded.

```
 1    #!/usr/local/bin/perl
 2
 3    # Simple error report generator for NCSA httpd error log files.
 4
 5    # A sample line from the NCSA http error log:
 6    # [Fri Jul  7 16:15:39 1995] httpd: send aborted for macmb.switch.ch
 7
 8    local (%count);
 9    local ($MAXMAILS) = 4;
10
11    # Open the error log file.
12    $errlog = "/hgdv/www/.logs/error_log";
```

```
13   open (FP, $errlog) || die ("$errlog: $!\n");
14
15   # Process it.
16   while ( <FP> ) {
17
18       # Message: "access failed".
19       if (/\[(([^\]]*)\] httpd: access to (.*) fail.*, reason: (.*)/){
20           $date = $1;
21           $file = $2;
22           $reason = $3;
23           if (-e $file
24               && $reason =~ "file permissions deny server access"){
25               &report_err ($file, $date, $reason);
26           }
27       }
28
29       # Message: "will not follow link".
30       if (/\[(([^\]]*)\] httpd: will not follow link (.*)/) {
31           $date = $1;
32           ($file = $2) =~ s/^\/wwwsrv/\/www/;
33           $reason = "symbolic link and link destination ".
34                     "have different owners";
35           if (-e $file) {
36               &report_err ($file, $date, $reason);
37           }
38       }
39   }
40
41   # Create an error report.
42   sub report_err {
43       local ($file, $date, $reason) = @_;
44       # Find out who owns the file...
45       local ($dev, $ino, $mode, $nlink, $uid, $gid, $rdev, $size,
46              $atime, $mtime, @dontcare) = stat($file);
47       # ... and get the user name.
48       local ($mailtext, $user);
49       $user = getpwuid($uid);
50
51       $mailtext = <<EOF;
52   Dear Sir or Madam,
53
54   this is to inform you that our Web server has encountered an
55   error while trying to serve the following file owned by you:
56   *** $file ***
57
58   Reason: $reason
59
60   (the webmasters)
61   THIS MAIL WAS AUTOMATICALLY SENT BY A SCRIPT - DO NOT REPLY
62   EOF
63       unless ( $user ) {
64           print STDERR ("could not get username for uid $uid\n");
65           return;
66       }
67
68       # Send mail message to the user.
69       print ("sending mail to $user\n");
70       if ( ++$count{$user} <= $MAXMAILS ) {
71           # Send no more than MAXMAILS.
72           print ("sending mail \#$count{$user} to $user\n");
73           &sendmail ($user, "Server error report", $mailtext);
74       }
75   }
```

A.3   Relational database interface

A.3.1   Listing: pl-sql.pl

This section contains the Perl code for a simple SQL interface. It works by passing SQL statements to an SQL interpreter and reading the interpreter's output. A simple database application can be written by including this code by means of the require statement. After setting the select, from, where, and order variables which represent their SQL equivalents, the function execsql() executes the SQL statement and returns the result as a list of attribute–value pairs.

```perl
1   #!/usr/local/bin/perl
2
3   # pl-sql.pl - simple SQL Interface for Perl - (queries only)
4
5   package perlsql;
6
7   &initsql ();
8
9   # execsql -- executes an SQL statement by forking off an
10  # SQL interpreter and parsing its output.
11  sub main'execsql {
12      local ($select, $from, $where, $order) = @_;
13      local ($result);
14
15      # Unbuffer stdout before forking and flush it.
16      select ((select(STDOUT),$|=1)[0]);
17      print ("");
18
19      $pid = open (FPIPE, "-|");
20      if ( $pid == 0 ) {
21          # Child process: call sql interpreter.
22          &sendsql ($select, $from, $where, $order);
23          exit;
24      }
25
26      # Parent process: post-process results.
27      while ( <FPIPE> ) {
28          local (%row) = ();
29          s/$DB_SPT/\n/g;
30          # For each row do...
31          foreach ( split (/\n/, $_) ) {
32              if ( m/(\S*)=(.*)$/ ) {
33                  # This might need massaging:
34                  $row{$1} = $2;
35                  $row{$1} =~ tr/\t / /s;
36                  $row{$1} =~ s/[ ]*$//g;
37                  $row{$1} =~ s/^[ ]*//g;
38              }
39              else {
40                  print STDERR ("pl-sql: no match ($_)\n");
41              }
42          }
43
44          foreach $field ( sort(keys(%row)) ) {
45              $value = $row{$field};
46              if ( length($value) > 0 ) {
47                  $result .= sprintf ("%-17s = '%s'\n",
48                                      $field, $value);
49              }
50              elsif ( length($field) > 0 ) {
51                  $result .= sprintf ("%-17s = '%s'\n",
52                                      $field, " ");
53              }
```

```
54              }
55
56              $result .= "\n";
57          }
58      close (FPIPE);
59      $result;
60  }
61
62  # sendsql -- call up an SQL Interpreter with a request.
63  # Note:
64  # the SQL statements usually need a lot of massaging
65  # before you get the desired output format.
66  sub sendsql {
67      local ($select, $from, $where, $order) = @_;
68      local (@fields) = split (/,/, $select);
69      open (FP, "| $sqlplus $sqlargs")
70          || die ("couldn't open pipe to sql interpreter: $!\n");
71      print FP ($sqlheader);
72      print FP ("select ");
73      foreach $i ( 0..$#fields ) {
74          local ($f) = $fields[$i];
75          unless ($i==0) { print FP (",\n"); }
76          print FP ("'$f=',$f,'$DB_SPT'");
77      }
78      print FP ("from $from\n");
79      print FP ("where $where\n");
80      print FP ("order $order\n");
81      print FP (";\n");
82      print FP ("exit;\n");
83      close (FP);
84  }
85
86  # initsql -- set sql initialisation, environment variables,
87  # paths, etc. This function must be modified to match whatever
88  # environment settings the specific sql interpreter requires.
89  # The example given here works with Oracle version 6.
90  sub initsql {
91      # Environment variables.
92      $ENV{"ORACLE_SID"} = "oracle6";
93      $ENV{"ORACLE_HOME"} = "/a3db1/oracle6";
94
95      # Path to interpreter and command line arguments.
96      $sqlplus = "/a3db1/oracle6/bin/sqlplus";
97      $sqlargs = "-s w3/w3";
98
99      # Sqlcommands that prefix the query.
100     $sqlheader = <<"END";
101     whenever sqlerror exit sql.sqlcode none;
102     set linesize 2000;
103     set flush off;
104     set feedback off;
105     set echo off;
106     set showmode off;
107     set heading off;
108     set verify off;
109     set arraysize 1;
110     set maxdata 32767;
111 END
112
113     # The character we use as a database seperator
114     # must not appear in any SQL tuple, but must
115     # be passed through by the SQL interpreter
116     # try "\007" (Bel), "\033" (Esc).
117     $DB_SPT = "\033";
118 }
119
```

A.3.2   Listing: `inquire.pl`

This section contains a sample application which makes use of the generic SQL
interface introduced in the previous section. In order to keep this example short
we have not built a forms interface around it.

```perl
1   #!/usr/local/bin/perl
2
3   # inquire.pl - sample use of SQL Interface for Perl
4
5   require "pl-sql.pl";
6
7   # Prepare sql statement.
8   $select = "last_name,first_name,affiliation";
9   $from = "chris.www_reg";
10  $order = "by last_name";
11  $where = "no_name_list is NULL and cancel_date is NULL";
12
13  # Execute sql statement.
14  $result = &execsql ($select, $from, $where, $order);
15
16  foreach $line ( split (/\n/, $result), "" ) {
17
18      # If line has the form "attribute=value"...
19      if ( $line =~ m/\s*(\S*)\s*=\s*' (.*)'/ ) {
20          # Store attribute and value in associative array.
21          $row{$1} = $2;
22          $isempty = 0;
23      }
24
25      # Empty line separates database rows -> print.
26      elsif ( $line =~ m/^$/ ) {
27          unless ( $isempty ) {
28              print ($row{"last_name"},";");
29              print ($row{"first_name"},";");
30              print ($row{"affiliation"},";");
31              print ($row{"email"},";\n");
32          }
33          $isempty = 1;
34          %row = ();
35      }
36      else {
37          print STDERR ("line doesn't match: [$line]\n");
38      }
39  }
40
```

A.4   Server indexing: meta-information

This section contains the complete code needed to enhance a server with a search
facility for document meta-information. Section 6.1.1 introduced HTML 2.0 compliant markup for including meta-information within hypertext documents. The
code from the following section extracts this information and builds a simple index
file. Section A.4.2 uses this index and provides a CGI compliant forms interface to
search this index file.

A.4.1   Listing: `meta-idx.pl`

This section contains code to build a server wide index from the HTML <META> tag.
In order to update the index at regular intervals, this function can be periodically
called using the Unix *cron* facility.

```perl
1   #!/usr/local/bin/perl
2
3   # meta-idx.pl - create a <META> tag index file
4
5   #--- start of configuration --- put your changes here ---
6   # The physical directory/directories to scan for html-files.
7   # Example:
8   #  @SEARCHDIRS=("/usr/www/dir/","/usr/foo/html-dir/");
9   @SEARCHDIRS = (
10    "/www/www95/papers",
11  );
12
13  # Location of the index file.
14  # Example:
15  #  $INDEXFILE="/usr/local/httpd/meta.idx"
16  $INDEXFILE = "/www/www95/meta.idx";
17  #--- end of configuration --- don't change anything below ---
18
19  require "find.pl";
20  local (@allfiles);
21
22  open (INDEX, ">$INDEXFILE")
23      || die ("Can't open $INDEXFILE: $!\n");
24  &find (@SEARCHDIRS); # find() will call wanted()
25
26  foreach $name ( @allfiles ) {
27      &indexfile ($name);
28  }
29
30  # Store name of HTML file in "@allfiles" (called by find).
31  sub wanted {
32      if ( /.html$/i ) {
33          push (@allfiles, $name);
34      }
35  }
36
37  # Parse file for META tags and store them in index.
38  sub indexfile {
39      local ($file) = @_;
40      local ($title, $intitle, $metaname, $metacont, @metalist);
41
42      unless (-r $file && open (FPIN,"$file") ) {
43          print STDERR ("Cannot read $file: $!\n");
44          return;
45      }
46
47      local ($dev, $ino, $mode, $nlink, $uid, $gid, $rdev, $size,
48              $atime, $mtime, @dontcare) = stat ($file);
49
50      # Set input separator to the tag close character ">".
51      $/ = ">";
52      while ( <FPIN> ) {
53          s/\s+/ /g;              # fold whitespaces into single blank
54          s/([^\n])</\1\n</g; # insert a CR before every '<'..
55          s/>([^\n])/>\n\1/g; # .. and after every '>'
56          foreach ( split (/\n/, $_) ) {
57              # Opening title tag.
58              if ( m:<title>:i ) {
59                  $intitle = 1;
60                  $title = "";
61                  next;
```

```
62                    }
63
64                    # Closing title tag.
65                    if(m:</title>:i){
66                        $intitle = 0;
67                        next;
68                    }
69
70                    # Meta element.
71                    if ( m:<meta name="(\S+)"\s+content="([^"]+)">:i ) {
72                        $metaname = $1;
73                        $metacont = $2;
74                        push (@metalist, "$metaname=$metacont");
75                        next;
76                    }
77
78                    # Title string.
79                    if ( $intitle && !/</ ) {
80                        $title .= $_;
81                    }
82                }
83            }
84
85        # If any meta tags were found...
86        if ( @metalist > 0 ) {
87            $file =~ tr/\n/ /s;
88            $title =~ tr/\n/ /s;
89            print INDEX ("\@f $file\n");
90            print INDEX ("\@t $title\n");
91            print INDEX ("\@m $mtime\n");
92            foreach $w ( @metalist ) {
93                print INDEX ("$w\n");
94            }
95        }
96        @metalist = ();
97        close (FPIN);
98    }
```

A.4.2   Listing: `meta-cgi.pl`

This section provides a CGI compliant interface to search an index to the information extracted from the <META> field in hypertext document headers.

```
1   #!/usr/local/bin/perl
2
3   # meta-cgi.pl - search in <META> tag index file
4
5   #--- start of configuration --- put your changes here ---
6   # Title or name of your server:
7   #    Example: $title="Search in Meta-Information";
8   $title = "Search in Meta-Information";
9
10  # Location of the indexfile:
11  #    Example: $indexfile="/usr/local/etc/httpd/index/index.idx";
12  $indexfile = "/tmp/meta.idx";
13
14  # URL Mappings (a.k.a Aliases) that your server does
15  # map "/" to some path to reflect a "document root"
16  #    Example
17  #    %urltopath = (
18  #      '/mms',    '/usr/stud/glaser/mms',
19  #      '/',       '/usr/www',
20  #    );
21
22  %urltopath = (
```

```
23    '/~neuss/',    '/Users/neuss/.htmlpub/',
24    '/',           '/Users',
25  );
26
27  # If you want the script to use GET rather then POST,
28  # comment out the following line:
29  $method = 'METHOD="POST"';
30
31  # There's a bug in NCSA httpd 1.4 which can require to hard code
32  # $scriptname instead of using the environment variable. If this
33  # is the case with your server setup, please change the line
34  # below.
35  $scriptname = $ENV{"SCRIPT_NAME"};
36  #--- end of configuration --- don't change anything below ---
37
38  &main();
39
40  sub send_index {
41      &send_header ();
42      &html_start ($title);
43      print ("<FORM $method ACTION=\"$scriptname\">\n");
44
45      print <<"ENDHTML";
46  <P>
47  Search field:
48  <SELECT NAME="Field">
49  <OPTION> Keywords
50  <OPTION> Author
51  <OPTION> Topic
52  </SELECT>
53  for expression: <INPUT NAME="value"   SIZE=20>
54  <P>
55  <INPUT TYPE="submit" VALUE="Search..">
56  <HR>
57  ENDHTML
58      &html_end;
59  }
60
61  # Get index entries matching query.
62  sub getmeta {
63      local ($attrib, $value) = @_;
64      local (%list, $grepexpr, $entry, $result);
65      $grepexpr = "^@|$attrib=.*$value.*";
66
67      local ($timstr);
68      open (FPIN,"<$indexfile") || die ("$indexfile: $!\n");
69      while ( <FPIN> ) {
70          next unless ( /^@|$grepexpr/io );
71          if ( /^@/ ) {
72              if ( /\@f\s(.*)$/ ) { $path  =$1; next; }
73              if ( /\@t\s(.*)$/ ) { $title =$1; next; }
74              if ( /\@m\s(.*)$/ ) { $mtime =$1; next; }
75          }
76          else {
77              local ($lastmod) = &timetostr ($mtime);
78              unless ($title) {
79                  $title="(NO TITLE)";
80              }
81              $path = &translateback ($path);
82              $entry = "<LI> <A HREF=\"$path\"><I>$title</I></A>";
83              $entry .= "<BR>\n";
84              $entry .= "$file (last change: $lastmod)<BR>\n";
85              $list{$path} = $entry;
86          }
87      }
88      local (@keys) = sort(keys(%list));
89      # If @keys is non-empty...
90      if ( @keys > 0 ) {
91          $result .= "<UL>\n";
```

```
92          foreach $key ( @keys ) {
93              $result .= $list{$key};
94          }
95          $result .= "</UL>\n";
96      }
97      else {
98          $result .= "(no match)\n";
99      }
100     $result;
101  }
102
103  # Translate URL to physical file name.
104  sub translate {
105      local ($url) = @_;
106      local ($docroot, $aliasdone);
107      $_ = $url;
108      s|/$||;        # strip off a trailing "/"
109      foreach $key ( keys(%urltopath) ) {
110          if ( $key eq "/" ) {
111              $docroot = $urltopath{$key};
112          }
113          if ( ($key ne "/") && (/^$key/) ) {
114              s/^$key/$urltopath{$key}/;
115              $aliasdone = 1;
116          }
117      }
118      if ( !$aliasdone && $docroot ) {
119          $_ = $docroot.$_;
120      }
121      $_;
122  }
123
124  # Translate physical name to URL.
125  sub translateback {
126      local ($url) = @_;
127      local ($docroot, $aliasdone);
128      $_ = $url;
129      s|/$||;        # strip off a trailing "/"
130      foreach $key ( keys(%urltopath) ) {
131          if ( $key eq "/" ) {
132              $docroot = $urltopath{$key};
133          }
134          else {
135              if ( /^$urltopath{$key}/ ) {
136                  s/^$urltopath{$key}/$key/;
137                  $aliasdone = 1;
138              }
139          }
140      }
141      if ( !$aliasdone && $docroot ) {
142          s/$docroot//;
143      }
144      $_;
145  }
146
147  sub main {
148
149      # If content_length is zero and query string is empty...
150      if ( ($ENV{CONTENT_LENGTH} == 0)
151          && (length($ENV{"QUERY_STRING"}) == 0) ) {
152          # We're not decoding a form yet => send the form.
153          &send_index ();
154          return;
155      }
156      else {
157          # Parse forms result and store it in an associative array.
158          %forms = &cgiparse ();
159      }
160
```

```
161    # Send content type header.
162    &send_header ();
163
164    # Send HTML code to the client.
165    &html_start ("$title - result");
166    print &getmeta ($forms{"attribute"}, $forms{"value"});
167    &html_end;
168  }
169
```

A.5   Client–server communication

This section contains Perl code for simple HTTP server and client applications. You can use this code as a basis for writing an automatic document retrieval utility, to compile 'what's new' lists, or even to combine server and client side code into your own gateway.

When writing automatic document retrieval programs, you should be aware that these programs can generate a heavy load on the servers they visit. Make sure that you are familiar with the conventions for HTTP robot programs[2].

A.5.1   Listing: `minisrv.pl`

This section contains a miniature but fully functional HTTP server.

```
1    #!/usr/local/bin/perl5
2
3    # miniserver.pl -- a miniature HTTP server.
4    #
5    # It serves documents from a fixed document root.
6    # Document types served are html and gif.
7    # Directories can be specified, it will try Welcome.html and
8    # index.html.
9    #
10   # To install, fill in your document root, copy the miniserver to
11   # some directory DIR, make it publicly executable, and add the
12   # following lines to your system config:
13   #
14   # /etc/services
15   #
16   #      ws                8080/tcp
17   #
18   # /etc/inetd.conf
19   #
20   #      ws   stream  tcp    nowait  nobody  DIR/miniserver      ws
21   #
22   # Send a 'kill -HUP' to your local inetd and you're set.
23
24   $docroot = '/var/spool/httpd/htdocs';
25   $version = 'HTTP/1.0';
26
27   # Read a line from STDIN, and discard the rest.
28   $request = <STDIN>;
29   while ( !eof(STDIN) ) {
30       $_ = <STDIN>;
31       # Blank line signals end of input.
32       last unless /\S/;
```

---

[2]http://web.nexor.co.uk/mak/doc/robots/robots.html

```
33   }
34
35   # Analyze the request.
36   if ( $request =~ m|^(\S+) (\S+) $version| ) {
37
38       $command = $1;
39       $request = $2;
40
41       # We only support the GET command.
42       &error (400, "Unknown command: $command")
43           unless $command eq 'GET';
44
45       # A little bit of security.
46       &error (404, "File $request not found")
47           if $request =~ m|/\.\.| || $request =~ m|\.\./|;
48
49       # Append filename to docroot.
50       $file = $docroot . '/' . $request;
51
52       # Check for a plain file.
53       if ( -f $file ) {
54           &send_file ($file);
55       }
56
57       # For a directory, try Welcome.html and index.html.
58       if ( -d $file ) {
59           # We cannot handle directory names without trailing slash
60           # unless we add code for redirections.
61           &error (404, "File $request not found")
62               unless $request =~ m|/$|;
63
64           if ( -s $file . '/Welcome.html' ) {
65               &send_file ($file . '/Welcome.html');
66           }
67           elsif ( -s $file . '/index.html' ) {
68               &send_file ($file . '/index.html');
69           }
70       }
71
72       # Fall through.
73       &error (404, "File $request not found");
74   }
75   &error (400, 'Unknown request');
76
77   sub send_file {
78       local ($file) = @_;
79
80       # We support two types: HTML docs and GIF files.
81       if ( $file =~ /\.html$/i ) {
82           print STDOUT ("$version 200 Document follows\n",
83                         "Content-Type: text/html\n",
84                         "\n");
85           open (F, $file);
86           print while <F>;
87           close (F);
88       }
89       elsif ( $file =~ /\.gif$/i ) {
90           print STDOUT ("$version 200 Document follows\n",
91                         "Content-Type: image/gif\n",
92                         "\n");
93           open (F, $file);
94           while ( ($cnt = sysread (F, $buf, 1024)) > 0 ) {
95               syswrite (STDOUT, $buf, $cnt);
96           }
97           close (F);
98       }
99       else {
100          &error (400, "Unknown filetype: $file");
101      }
```

```
102        exit (0);
103    }
104
105    sub error {
106        local ($num, $msg) = @_;
107        print STDOUT ("$version $num $msg\n",
108                      "Content-Type: text/html\n",
109                      "\n",
110                      "<h1>Error $num: $msg</h1>\n");
111        exit (0);
112    }
```

A.5.2 Listing: `get-http.pl`

Here is code for a routine that connects to a remote HTTP server and retrieves a
given URL. It can be very useful for writing a robot that calls up a gateway program
and passes it arguments.

```
1   #!/usr/local/bin/perl
2
3   # Connect to remote server and perform HTTP method.
4   # Based on geturl() by Dan Grillo, NeXT. Used with permission.
5
6   # get_http() allows you to connect to a remote server and
7   # perform a request using one of the following HTTP methods:
8   # GET, POST, or HEAD.
9   #
10  # If a "query" argument is provided, the query is encoded
11  # appropriately with the request. This can be very useful
12  # when automatically connecting to a remote CGI script.
13  #
14  # Please note that the query must be complient to the HTTP
15  # standard, i.e. variables and filenames must be properly
16  # URL encoded. This cannot be done inside get-http without
17  # compromising the ability to call remote CGI scripts.
18  #
19  # The following example simulates a forms query by connecting
20  # to the URL http://calliope.lahn.de/cgi-neuss/searchm.pl and
21  # using the POST protocol element to supply the values
22  # "Field=Subject" and "Expr=WWW" to the CGI script:
23
24  #       $remote = "calliope.lahn.de";
25  #       $file = "/cgi-neuss/searchm.pl";
26  #       $method = "POST";
27  #       $port = 80;
28  #       $query = "Field=Subject&Expr=WWW";
29  #       print &get_http($remote,$method,$file,$port,$query);
30
31  package get_http;
32
33  # get_http ($remote, $method, $file, $port, $query)
34  #
35  sub main'get_http {
36      local ($remote, $method, $file, $port, $query) = @_;
37
38      $contlen = length ($query);
39
40      # POST: send "Content-Length", followed by query string
41      if ( $method eq "POST" ) {
42          $request = "$method $file HTTP/1.0\n";
43          $request .= "Content-Length: $contlen\n";
44          $request .= "\n$query";
45      }
46
47      # GET/HEAD: append encoded query to $file path
```

```
48      elsif ( $method eq "GET" || $method eq "HEAD" ) {
49          $request  = "$method $file";
50          if($contlen>0){
51              $request  .= "?$query HTTP/1.0\n\n";
52          }
53      }
54
55      # Unknown method: print error message and die.
56      else {
57          die ("unsupported HTTP method '$method'\n");
58      }
59
60      # Use default port unless otherwise specified.
61      unless ($port) { $port=80; }
62
63      &get_request ($remote, $port, $request);
64  }
65
66  # Interrupt handler.
67  sub dokill {
68      kill (9, $child) if $child;
69  }
70
71  # get_request ($server, $port, $request)
72  #
73  sub get_request {
74      local ($server, $port, $request) = @_;
75      local (@page); # will hold the result of the request
76
77      # Some predefined values.
78      $AF_INET = 2;
79      $SOCK_STREAM = 1;
80
81      # Set interrupt handler (to handle e.g. a Ctrl-C).
82      $SIG{'INT'} = 'dokill';
83
84      # Get the hostname, chop trailing newline.
85      chop ($hostname = 'hostname');
86
87      ($name, $aliases, $proto) = getprotobyname ('tcp');
88
89      # Get local and remote host address.
90      ($name, $aliases, $type, $len, $thisaddr)
91          = gethostbyname ($hostname);
92      ($name, $aliases, $type, $len, $thataddr)
93          = gethostbyname ($server);
94
95      # Pack into internal format.
96      $sockaddr = 'S n a4 x8';
97      $this = pack ($sockaddr, $AF_INET, 0, $thisaddr);
98      $that = pack ($sockaddr, $AF_INET, $port, $thataddr);
99
100     # Create a socket, bind to a name, and open connection.
101     socket (S, $AF_INET, $SOCK_STREAM, $proto)
102         || die ("socket: $!\n");
103     bind (S, $this) || die ("bind: $!\n");
104     connect (S, $that) || die ("connect: $!\n");
105
106     # Set I/O on filehandle S to non-buffered.
107     select((select(S), $| = 1)[0]); # yeah, its cryptic..
108
109     # Execute request by piping it to the socket.
110     print S ("$request");
111     @page = <S>;
112     close (S);
113
114     # return result
115     @page;
116 }
```

A.6   Using `CGI.pm`

`CGI.pm` is a Perl 5 module, written by Lincoln D. Stein, that provides powerful tools for gateway programs. The following sample program demonstrates most of the features discussed earlier in the book:

- Dynamic generation of forms data.

- Maintaining state using hidden fields.

- Advanced error handling.

- A user-friendly interface.

The program constructs an initial form when called without any form data. If it is passed form data, this is analyzed and mailed to the Web administrator. If errors are detected, a new form is generated similar to the original one. The data that was submitted is used to initialize the fields of the new form with error messages marking the fields that were in error. To make corrections, the user need not navigate back to the original form, but can use the newly presented form.

Important: This is the only example program that requires Perl version 5 or later. You may have to change the first line of the program if your Perl is not version 5 (for example `/usr/local/bin/perl5`). Also, you have to install the module `CGI.pm`, which can be found on the CDROM, in a place where Perl can find it, usually `/usr/local/lib/perl5`.

A.6.1   Listing: `order.pl`

```
1   #!/usr/local/bin/perl
2
3   # Order form using CGI.pm lib.
4   # >>>> THIS PROGRAM REQUIRES PERL VERSION 5 <<<<
5
6   use CGI;
7
8   ############### Presets ###############
9
10  $mailto = "webmaster\@master.web";
11
12  ############### The Process ###############
13
14  # Allocate new query and initialize.
15  $query = new CGI;
16  &banner;
17  if ( $query->param('form_filled') ) {
18      if ( &handle_form ) {
19          &ok;
20          exit (0);
21      }
22      &build_form (0);
23  }
24  else {
25      &build_form (1);
26  }
27  exit (0);
28
```

```
29   ############### Subroutines ###############
30
31   sub banner {
32       print $query->header;
33       print $query->start_html('Order Form');
34       print STDOUT ("<body>\n",
35                      "<h2>Order Form</h2>\n",
36                      "<hr>",
37                      "<p>\n");
38   }
39
40   sub handle_form {
41       local ($err) = 0;
42
43       $err++, $flag{'Company'} = 'Company name is missing'
44           unless $query->param('Company');
45       $err++, $flag{'Name'} = 'Name is missing'
46           unless $query->param('Name');
47       $err++, $flag{'Address'} = 'Incomplete address'
48           unless $query->param('Address');
49       $err++, $flag{'Zipcode'} = 'Incomplete address'
50           unless $query->param('Zipcode');
51       $err++, $flag{'City'} = 'Incomplete address'
52           unless $query->param('City');
53       $err++, $flag{'E-Mail'} = 'E-mail address is missing'
54           unless $query->param('E-Mail');
55       $err++, $flag{'E-Mail'} = 'Incorrect E-mail address'
56           unless $query->param('E-Mail') =~ /.+\@.+/;
57
58       if ( $err ) {
59           print STDOUT ("<strong>\n",
60                          "Please verify the data ",
61                          "and try again.\n",
62                          "</strong>\n");
63           return 0;
64       }
65
66       1;
67   }
68
69   sub ok {
70
71       $SIG{'PIPE'} = 'IGNORE';
72       open (MAIL, "|/usr/lib/sendmail -t")
73           || print STDERR ("mailin: $!\n");
74
75       print MAIL ("To: $mailto\n",
76                    "From: WWW Server <webmaster>\n",
77                    "Subject: Order query\n");
78       print MAIL ("\n");
79
80       print MAIL ("\n",
81       "Date     : ". localtime(time), "\n\n",
82       "Company  : ", $query->param('Company'), "\n",
83       "Name     : ", $query->param('Name'), "\n",
84       "Address  : ", $query->param('Address'), "\n",
85       "Zipcode  : ", $query->param('Zipcode'), "\n",
86       "City     : ", $query->param('City'), "\n",
87       "Country  : ", $query->param('Country'), "\n",
88       "Phone    : ", $query->param('Telephone'), "\n",
89       "Fax      : ", $query->param('Fax'), "\n",
90       "E-mail   : ", $query->param('E-Mail'), "\n");
91
92       close (MAIL);
93       print STDERR ("mailin: $!\n") if $?;
94
95       print STDOUT ("\n",
96                      "Thank you for entering your data.\n");
97       print $query->end_html;
```

```
98   }
99
100  sub build_form {
101      local ($new) = @_;
102      print $query->startform;
103      print <<EOD if $new;
104  Please fill in the right data so we can add you to our
105  mailinglist.
106
107  EOD
108      print "<pre>";
109      print ("       Company: ",
110              $query->textfield('Company',undef,30),
111              &rightorwrong($new,'Company'), "\n");
112      print ("          name: ",
113              $query->textfield('Name',undef,30),
114              &rightorwrong($new,'Name'), "\n");
115      print ("       address: ",
116              $query->textfield('Address',undef,30),
117              &rightorwrong($new,'Address'), "\n");
118      print ("       zipcode: ",
119              $query->textfield('Zipcode',undef,10),
120              &rightorwrong($new,'Zipcode'), "\n");
121      print ("          city: "
122              , $query->textfield('City',undef,30),
123              &rightorwrong($new,'City'), "\n");
124      print ("       country: ",
125              $query->textfield('Country',undef,30),
126              &rightorwrong($new), "\n");
127      print ("\n");
128      print ("         phone: ",
129              $query->textfield('Telephone',undef,15),
130              &rightorwrong($new), "\n");
131      print ("           fax: ",
132              $query->textfield('Fax',undef,15),
133              &rightorwrong($new), "\n");
134      print ("        E-mail: ",
135              $query->textfield('E-Mail',undef,30),
136              &rightorwrong($new,'E-Mail'), "\n");
137      print <<EOD;
138  </pre>
139  <hr>
140  EOD
141      print $query->submit('Submit');
142      print <<EOD;
143  <p>
144  <hr>
145  EOD
146      print $query->hidden('form_filled','true');
147      print $query->endform;
148      print $query->end_html;
149  }
150
151  sub rightorwrong {
152      local ($new, $which) = @_;
153      return if $new;
154      return ""
155          if !defined $which || !defined $flag{$which};
156      return "  <b>This field may not be left blank</b>"
157          unless $query->param($which);
158      return "  <b>".$flag{$which}."</b>";
159  }
```

A.7   File locking using `fcntl`

In Section 5.2.4 we have implemented file locking using the Unix *flock* system call. The following Perl code defines a subroutine `lockfile` that handles file locking using the Unix *fcntl* system call. This routine can be used in situations where *flock* is not available.

```
1    # Subroutine lockfile:
2    #
3    #    &lockfile (FH)
4    #
5    #    FH is a handle to an opened file, with r/w access.
6    #
7    # Return values:
8    #    1   lock succeeded
9    #    0   lock failed
10   #
11   # Locking is implemented using the fcntl(2) system call that is
12   # available on most modern systems.
13   #
14   # Typical use:
15   #
16   #    open (F, "+>>datafile") || die (...);
17   #    if ( &lockfile (F) ) {
18   #       seek (F, 0, 2);      # seek to end
19   #       print F (...);       # append info
20   #    }
21   #    close (F);              # release the file and lock
22
23   sub lockfile {
24       local ($FH) = @_;
25
26       require "fcntl.ph";
27
28       local ($func) = &F_SETLKW;          # set lock and wait for it
29       local ($lck) =
30           pack ("sslli",   # see man for flock(2)
31                 &F_WRLCK,  # short l_type (F_WRLCK: write lock)
32                 0,         # short l_whence (as in lseek(2))
33                 0,         # long l_start (start of region)
34                 0,         # long l_len (0 -> whole file)
35                 0);        # int l_pid (not used)
36       local ($ret) = fcntl ($FH, $func, $lck);
37       return 1 if $ret eq "0 but true";
38       0;                       # failed
39   }
40
```

At line 26 the file `fnctl.ph` is `required` from the Perl library. This file contains the definitions of `F_SETLKW` and `F_WRLCK` needed for the `fcntl` system call. Note that the file `fcntl.ph` is not part of the standard Perl distribution and must be created using the *h2ph* program that comes with Perl. Also note that `fcntl.ph` usually requires some other files which may require other files and so on. It may take a couple of attempts before all the necessary files are created and available.

Lines 28–35 contains the code to construct the necessary parameters for `fcntl`. As described in the Perl documentation, `fcntl` returns a '0 but true' result upon success, which is checked at line 37. If the lock cannot be set the routine returns zero.

Appendix B

CDROM contents

A CDROM, such as the one that accompanies this book, is capable of holding over 600Mb of data. We have not attempted to fill our CDROM, but have limited ourselves to information we consider particularly relevant to the book:

- Sample code for both simple scripts and the more sophisticated gateway programs discussed in this book.

- All Web references from the book.

- Third party distribution of free software packages and files, that are used by the examples and sample programs.

The easiest way to read the CDROM is by means of a Web browser. The root directory contains an HTML document 'index.html' that guides you through the contents of the disk.

B.1   Examples from this book

All the examples, sample scripts and programs from this book are available on the CDROM. They are also available on the International Thomsom Web server[1]. In future, we will update the examples and other information on this server as necessary.

The CDROM contains a directory 'book', which in turn contains subdirectories for each of the chapters of the book. The example programs on the CDROM are exact copies of the programs from the book. In fact, they have been generated automatically from the document sources of the book to guarantee conformance.

In Chapter 5 we discussed subroutines for common tasks performed by gateway programs. Normally, such utility functions are put into an external file, which is then included in the Perl programs with a `require` statement. On the CDROM in

---

[1]http://www.thomson.com/itcp/

directory 'ch05' you will find a file 'libgw.pl' that contains all the subroutines suitable for inclusion. However, in order to make it easier to run the example programs, they already include all the necessary subroutines. The example programs from Appendix A 'Commented listings' can be found in directory 'appendix'.

B.2   Web references

This book contains numerous references to items on the Web, given in the form of URLs. On the CDROM you will find an HTML document, 'hotlist.html', which contains all these references as hyperlinks. Instead of typing them just point and click! Of course, the most up-to-date version of the hot-list will also be available from the Thomson server.

B.3   Free utilities and files

Several software packages and other information that can make the life of a webmaster easier are located in the directory '3rd-part'. We have included two formats, a DOS compliant '8.3' version, to make it easier to put the files on a floppy disk, and an unpacked version for direct use on Unix, Macintosh, Microsoft Windows or Windows NT machines.

Note that 'free' does *not* imply that the packages are in the public domain. Some of them have copyrights or other restrictions attached. They can, however, be used freely and are included on the CDROM with permission of the respective authors.

CGI.pm

The CGI.pm library lets you create Web fill-out forms during processing and parse the data returned by them. You can parse CGI queries, create forms, and maintain the state of the forms input fields and buttons between two forms invocations. The library, which is written in Perl 5 by Lincoln D. Stein, handles both POST and GET methods correctly, and can also decode input provided via the <ISINDEX> method. It includes a command line debugging facility, which facilitates the development and testing of gateway programs without running them under a server or manually setting environment variables.

For more information about CGI.pm, and the most recent version, see:

```
http://www-genome.wi.mit.edu/ftp/pub/software/WWW/cgi_docs.html
```

cgi-lib.pl

The CGI forms handling library was written by Steven Brenner. Unlike CGI.pm, it does not require Perl 5, but will also run under Perl version 4. It provides functions that decode forms input, print HTTP compliant headers, create error messages, and distinguish between POST and GET requests. The software can be obtained from:

```
http://www.bio.cam.ac.uk/web/form.html
```

`libwww-perl`

The `libwww-perl` library of Perl routines provides a programming interface to the Web. It contains various routines that come in especially useful when writing HTTP clients and HTML processors.

The library contains:

- A simple program for performing GET requests from the command-line.

- Routines for link extraction.

- A package for implementing the robot exclusion protocol.

- Utilities for reading and manipulating HTML documents.

- Utilities for handling MIME `mailcap` files and executing viewers by their Content-Type.

Information on `libwww-perl` can be found at:

```
http://www.ics.uci.edu/pub/websoft/libwww-perl
```

The most recent version of the software can be found at the same location.

The GD graphics library

The GD graphics library was written by Thomas Boutell while working at Cold Spring Harbor Labs. It is copyright 1994, 1995, Quest Protein Database Center, Cold Spring Harbor Labs. GD may be copied and distributed freely provided that credit is given in all derived works.

The library provides C routines for creating, reading, writing, and manipulating GIF graphics files. It provides features for:

- Drawing lines, rectangles, arcs, ellipses and text.

- Combining multiple images to form new ones.

- Flood filling of shapes.

- Filling of shapes with tiled patterns.

- Creating interlaced images.

The GD library can be obtained at:

```
http://siva.cshl.org/gd/gd.html
```

GD.pm

GD.pm is a port of the GD library by Lincoln Stein. It has the same features as the original C library, but takes advantage of Perl's object oriented features by defining the following classes:

GD::Image
  An image class that represents the image data and accepts graphic primitive method calls.

GD::Font
  A font class that holds static font information to be used for text rendering.

GD::Polygon
  A simple polygon object used for storing lists of vertices prior to rendering a polygon into an image.

The GD.pm library can be obtained from:

    ftp://ftp-genome.wi.mit.edu/pub/software/WWW/GD.pm.tar.Z

Information on the latest developments is kept at:

    http://www-genome.wi.mit.edu/ftp/pub/software/WWW/GD.html

B.4   Internet Domain Codes

An Internet domain name or mail address such as jv@squirrel.org ends in a so called *top-level domain name* such as .com or .org. This top-level domain name can refer to a country or a functional code which classifies the type of organization. Table B.1 lists some of the most common functional codes.

Table B.1   Common top-level domain names

Name	Meaning
.com	commercial organizations
.edu	educational institutions
.gov	US government
.mil	US military
.net	Internet network services
.org	non-profit organizations

The country codes adhere to the ISO 3166 standard for the representation of names of countries. It defines two-letter codes such as AD for Andorra, AE for the United Arab Emirates, and so on. A list of domain codes permits Internet addresses to be listed by the name of the country, something that can be quite useful when writing a log analysis utility, for example.

B.5 Frequently asked questions

The World Wide Web FAQ

The World Wide Web FAQ contains a compilation of frequently asked questions and answers on World Wide Web related topics. It is maintained by Thomas Boutell and can be retrieved from:

```
http://sunsite.unc.edu/boutell/faq/faq.tar.Z
```

The Perl FAQ

The Perl FAQ is a list of the most frequently asked questions (with answers) from comp.lang.perl, a Usenet newsgroup devoted to the Perl programming language. It is maintained by Tom Christiansen and Stephen P. Potter and posted at regular intervals to the comp.lang.perl.announce newsgroup. It can also be obtained from:

```
ftp://rtfm.mit.edu/pub/usenet/comp.lang.perl/
```

A version which has been converted to HTML can be found on:

```
http://scwww.ucs.indiana.edu/FAQ/Perl/
```

The HTML version of the Perl FAQ is maintained by the Indiana University Support Center.

Appendix C

Resources not on the CDROM

Many useful resources have not been reproduced in full on the CDROM, but are available via hyperlinks.

All the hyperlinks in this section can be found in the file 'hotlist.html' on the CDROM.

C.1 Files and utilities available free of charge

Perl

The 'Comprehensive Perl Archive Network' has been formed to coordinate the wide-spread distribution of Perl. All sites participating in the CPAN have the same files available. For further information about Perl and how to get it, see:

    http://www.perl.com

The Perl programming language is adopted by the GNU project of the Free Software Foundation and can be found on all FTP sites that mirror GNU software.

Tcl/Tk

Tcl (tool command language) is an embeddable scripting language and Tk is a graphical user interface toolkit based on Tcl. For more information:

    http://www.sunlabs.com/research/tcl/

Python

Python is an interpreted, interactive, object oriented programming language. Information can be found on:

    http://www.python.org/

Icon

Icon is a high-level, general-purpose programming language with a large repertoire of features for processing data structures and character strings. It is an imperative, procedural language with a syntax reminiscent of C and Pascal, but with semantics at a much higher level. For more information, see:

```
http://www.cs.arizona.edu/icon/www/index.html
```

Mosaic

NCSA Mosaic is a networked information discovery, retrieval, and collaboration tool and World Wide Web browser. It is a part of NCSA's Mosaic project. Mosaic is free for non-commercial use and runs on Unix (using the X Window System), Microsoft Windows, Windows NT and Macintosh. For more information see:

```
http:http://www.ncsa.uiuc.edu/SDG/Software/Mosaic/
```

Netscape Navigator

Netscape Navigator is a very popular commercial Web browser program, which can be tried free of charge. Information is available on:

```
http://www.mcom.com
```

CERN Web Server

The CERN server is a free Web server that runs on Unix, Windows NT and VMS. For more information, see:

```
http://www.w3.org/pub/WWW/Daemon/
```

C.2   Mailing lists

Several mailing lists exist that carry valuable information. All of the following mailing lists can be subscribed to by sending a electronic mail message containing the word 'SUBSCRIBE' to the addresses indicated.

Perl Porters <perl5-porters-request@nicoh.com>

In theory, people porting Perl to other platforms, but in practice, often the Perl developers mailing list.

Perl Packrats <perl-packrats-request@metronet.com>

People who keep Perl archives.

CGI Perl `<CGI-perl-request@webstorm.com>`

Developers' mailing list for those working on Perl CGI modules. This is not a list for requesting help in using Perl for CGI programming.

LibWWW list `<libwww-perl-request@ics.UCI.EDU>`

People working on modules using the WWW protocols directly.

WWW Security `<www-security-request@nsmx.rutgers.edu>`

A working group discussing security issues.

C.3   Usenet Newsgroups

comp.lang.perl.announce

Announcements about new Perl versions, new modules and so on.

comp.lang.perl.misc

Everything you want to know about Perl.

comp.infosystems.www.authoring.cgi

Discussion forum for authors of CGI compliant gateway programs.

Appendix D

Perl Reference Guide

This section contains a reprint of the Perl 5 Reference Guide as designed by Johan Vromans. It is included with permission of the author.

A PostScript file containing a neatly formatted version of this Reference Guide can be downloaded from the International Thomson Web server[1]. Printed copies can be ordered from ITP.

---

[1] http://www.thomson.com/itcp/WebExtra/

Contents

Conventions

`fixed`   denotes literal text.

THIS   means variable text, i.e. things you must fill in.

THIS†   means that **THIS** will default to `$_` if omitted.

word   is a keyword, i.e. a word with a special meaning.

`RET`   denotes pressing a keyboard key.

[...]   denotes an optional part.

Command line options

`-a`   turns on autosplit mode when used with `-n` or `-p`. Splits to `@F`.

`-c`   checks syntax but does not execute.

`-d`   runs the script under the debugger. Use '`-de   0`' to start the debugger without a script.

-D **NUMBER**
sets debugging flags.

-e **COMMANDLINE**
to enter a single line of script. Multiple `-e` commands may be given to build up a multi-line script.

-F **REGEXP**
specifies a regular expression to split on if `-a` is in effect.

-i **EXT**
files processed by the `<>` construct are to be edited in-place.

-I **DIR**
with `-P`: tells the C preprocessor where to look for include files. The directory is prepended to `@INC`.

-l [**OCTNUM**]
enables automatic line ending processing, e.g. `-1013`.

`-n`   assumes an input loop around the script. Lines are not printed.

`-p`   assumes an input loop around the script. Lines are printed.

`-P`   runs the C preprocessor on the script before compilation by Perl.

`-s`   interprets '`-xxx`' on the command line as switches and sets the corresponding variables `$xxx` in the script.

`-S`   uses the `PATH` environment variable to search for the script.

-T   forces *taint* checking.

-u   dumps core after compiling the script. To be used with the *undump* program (where available).

-U   allows Perl to perform unsafe operations.

-v   prints the version and patchlevel of your Perl executable.

-w   prints warnings about possible spelling errors and other error-prone constructs in the script.

-x [**DIR**]
      extracts Perl program from the input stream. If **DIR** is specified, switches to this directory before running the program.

-0 **VAL**
      (that's the number zero) designates an initial value for the record separator $/. See also -1.

Literals

Numeric: 123   1_234   123.4   5E-10   0xff (hex)   0377 (octal).

String: 'abc' literal string, no variable interpolation nor escape characters, except \' and \\. Also: q/abc/. Almost any pair of delimiters can be used instead of /.../.

"abc" Variables are interpolated and escape sequences are processed. Also: qq/abc/.
Escape sequences: \t (Tab), \n (Newline), \r (Return), \f (Formfeed), \b (Backspace), \a (Alarm), \e (Escape), \033(octal), \x1b(hex), \c[(control).
\l and \u lowcase/upcase the following character;
\L and \U lowcase/upcase until a \E is encountered.
\Q quote regexp characters until a \E is encountered.

'COMMAND' evaluates to the output of the **COMMAND**. Also: qx/**COMMAND**/.

Array: (1,2,3). () is an empty array.
(1..4) is the same as (1,2,3,4). Likewise ('abc'..'ade').
qw/foo bar.../ is the same as ('foo','bar',...).

Array reference: [1,2,3].

Hash (associative array): (KEY1, VAL1, KEY2, VAL2, ...).
Also: (KEY1 => VAL1, KEY2 => VAL2, ...).

Hash reference: {KEY1, VAL1, KEY2, VAL2, ...}.

Code reference: **sub** { STATEMENTS }

Filehandles: STDIN, STDOUT, STDERR, ARGV, DATA.
   User-specified: **HANDLE**, $VAR.

Globs: <PATTERN> evaluates to all filenames according to the pattern.
   Use '<${VAR}>' or '**glob** $VAR' to glob from a variable.

Here-Is: <<IDENTIFIER   *See the Perl manual for details.*

Special tokens:
   __FILE__: filename; __LINE__: line number.
   __END__: end of program; remaining lines can be read using <DATA>.

Variables

$var	a simple scalar variable.
$var[28]	29th element of array @var.
$p = \@var	now $p is a reference to array @var.
$$p[28]	29th element of array referenced by $p. Also: $p->[28].
$var[-1]	last element of array @var.
$var[$i][$j]	$j-th element of $i-th element of array @var.
$var{'Feb'}	a value from 'hash' (associative array) %var.
$p = \%var	now $p is a reference to hash %var.
$$p{'Feb'}	a value from hash referenced by $p. Also: $p->{'Feb'}.
$#var	last index of array @var.
@var	the entire array; in a scalar context: the number of elements in the array.
@var[3,4,5]	a slice of array @var.
@var{'a','b'}	a slice of %var; same as ($var{'a'},$var{'b'}).
%var	the entire hash; in a scalar context: **true** if the hash has elements.

$var{'a',1,...} emulates a multi-dimensional array.

('a'..'z')[4,7,9] a slice of an array literal.

PKG::VAR	a variable from a package, e.g. $pkg::var, @pkg::ary.
\OBJECT	reference to an object, e.g. \$var, \%hash.
***NAME**	refers to all objects represented by **NAME**. '*n1 = *n2' makes n1 an alias for n2. '*n1 = \$n2' makes $n1 an alias for $n2.

You can always use a { **BLOCK** } returning the right type of reference instead of the variable identifier, e.g. ${...}, &{...}. $$p is just a shorthand for ${$p}.

Operators

**	Exponentiation.
+ - * /	Addition, subtraction, multiplication, division.
%	Modulo division.
& | ^	Bitwise AND, bitwise OR, bitwise exclusive OR.
>> <<	Bitwise shift right, bitwise shift left.
|| &&	Logical OR, logical AND.
.	Concatenation of two strings.
x	Returns a string or array consisting of the left operand (an array or a string) repeated the number of times specified by the right operand.

All of the above operators also have an associated assignment operator, e.g. '.='.

->	Dereference operator.
\	Reference (unary).
! ~	Negation (unary), bitwise complement (unary).
++ --	Auto-increment (magical on strings), auto-decrement.
== !=	Numeric equality, inequality.
eq ne	String equality, inequality.
< >	Numeric less than, greater than.
lt gt	String less than, greater than.
<= >=	Numeric less (greater) than or equal to.
le ge	String less (greater) than or equal.
<=> **cmp**	Numeric (string) compare. Returns -1, 0 or 1.
=~ !~	Search pattern, substitution, or translation (negated).
..	Bistable (scalar context) or enumeration (array context).
? :	Alternation (if-then-else) operator.
,	Comma operator, also list element separator. You can also use =>.
not	low-precedence negation.
and	low-precedence and.
or xor	low-precedence or, xor.

A 'list' is a list of expressions, variables or lists. An array variable or an array slice may always be used instead of a list.

All Perl functions can be used as list operators, in which case they have very high or very low precedence, depending on whether you look at the left side of the operator or at the right side of it.

Only the operators **not**, **and**, **or** and **xor**, have lower precedence.

Parentheses can always be added around the parameter lists to avoid problems.

Statements

Every statement is an expression, optionally followed by a modifier, and terminated with a semicolon. The semicolon may be omitted if the statement is the final one in a **BLOCK**.

Execution of expressions can depend on other expressions using one of the modifiers **if**, **unless**, **while** or **until**, e.g.:

```
EXPR1 if EXPR2 ;
EXPR1 until EXPR2 ;
```

Also, by using one of the logical operators | |, && or ? :, e.g.:

```
EXPR1 | | EXPR2 ;
EXPR1 ? EXPR2 : EXPR3 ;
```

Statements can be combined to form a **BLOCK** when enclosed in {}. **BLOCK**s may be used to control flow:

```
if (EXPR) BLOCK [[ elsif (EXPR) BLOCK ... ] else BLOCK ]
unless (EXPR) BLOCK [ else BLOCK ]
[ LABEL: ] while (EXPR) BLOCK [ continue BLOCK ]
[ LABEL: ] until (EXPR) BLOCK [ continue BLOCK ]
[ LABEL: ] for ( [ EXPR ] ; [ EXPR ] ; [ EXPR ] ) BLOCK
[ LABEL: ] foreach VAR† (ARRAY) BLOCK
[ LABEL: ] BLOCK [ continue BLOCK ]
```

Program flow can be controlled with:

goto LABEL
>   Continue execution at the specified label.

last [LABEL]
>   Immediately exits the loop in question. Skips continue block.

next [LABEL]
>   Starts the next iteration of the loop.

redo [LABEL]
>   Restarts the loop block without evaluating the conditional again.

Special forms are:

```
do BLOCK while EXPR ;
do BLOCK until EXPR ;
```

which are guaranteed to perform **BLOCK** once before testing **EXPR**, and

```
do BLOCK
```

which effectively turns **BLOCK** into an expression.

Subroutines, packages and modules

&SUBROUTINE LIST
>   Executes a **SUBROUTINE** declared by a **sub** declaration, and returns the value

of the last expression evaluated in **SUBROUTINE** .

SUBROUTINE can be an expression yielding a reference to a code object. The & may be omitted if the subroutine has been declared before being used.

bless REF [, PACKAGE]

Turns the object **REF** into an object in **PACKAGE**. Returns the reference.

caller [EXPR]

Returns an array ($package,$file,$line,...) for a specific subroutine call. 'caller' returns this info for the current subroutine, 'caller(1)' for the caller of this subroutine etc.. Returns **false** if no caller.

do SUBROUTINE LIST

Deprecated form of &SUBROUTINE

goto &SUBROUTINE

Substitutes a call to **SUBROUTINE** for the current subroutine.

import MODULE [LIST]

Imports the named subroutines from **MODULE**.

no MODULE [LIST]

Cancels imported semantics. See **use**.

package NAME

Designates the remainder of the current block as a package.

require EXPR†

If **EXPR** is numeric, requires Perl to be at least that version. Otherwise **EXPR** must be the name of a file that is included from the Perl library. Does not include more than once, and yields a fatal error if the file does not evaluate to a **true** value.

If **EXPR** is a bare word, assumes extension '.pm' for the name of the file.

return EXPR

Returns from a subroutine with the value specified.

sub NAME { EXPR ; ... }

Designates **NAME** as a subroutine. Parameters are passed by reference as array @_. Returns the value of the last expression evaluated.

[**sub**] BEGIN { EXPR ; ... }

Defines a setup **BLOCK** to be called before execution.

[**sub**] END { EXPR ; ... }

Defines a cleanup **BLOCK** to be called upon termination.

tie VAR, PACKAGE, [LIST]

Ties a variable to a package that will handle it. Can be used to bind a dbm or ndbm file to a hash.

untie VAR
>   Breaks the binding between the variable and the package.

use MODULE [LIST]
>   Imports semantics from the named module into the current package.

Object oriented programming

Perl rules of object oriented programming:

• An object is simply a reference that happens to know which class it belongs to. Objects are blessed, references are not.

• A class is simply a package that happens to provide methods to deal with object references.
  If a package fails to provide a method, the base classes as listed in @ISA are searched.

• A method is simply a subroutine that expects an object reference (or a package name, for static methods) as the first argument.
  Methods can be applied with:
>   METHOD OBJREF PARAMETERS   or
>   OBJREF->METHOD PARAMETERS

Arithmetic functions

abs EXPR†
>   Returns the absolute value of its operand.

atan2 Y, X
>   Returns the arctangent of Y/X in the range $-\pi$ to π.

cos EXPR†
>   Returns the cosine of EXPR (expressed in radians).

exp EXPR†
>   Returns e to the power of EXPR.

int EXPR†
>   Returns the integer portion of EXPR.

log EXPR†
>   Returns natural logarithm (base e) of EXPR.

rand [EXPR]
>   Returns a random fractional number between 0 and the value of EXPR. If EXPR is omitted, returns a value between 0 and 1.

sin EXPR†

Returns the sine of **EXPR** (expressed in radians).

sqrt EXPR†

Returns the square root of **EXPR**.

srand [EXPR]

Sets the random number seed for the rand operator.

time   Returns the number of seconds since January 1, 1970. Suitable for feeding to **gmtime** and **localtime**.

Conversion functions

chr EXPR†

Returns the character represented by the decimal value **EXPR**.

gmtime EXPR†

Converts a time as returned by the **time** function to a 9-element array (0:$sec, 1:$min, 2:$hour, 3:$mday, 4:$mon, 5:$year, 6:$wday, 7:$yday, 8:$isdst) with the time analyzed for the Greenwich time zone. $mon has the range 0..11 and $wday has the range 0..6.

hex EXPR†

Returns the decimal value of **EXPR** interpreted as an hex string.

localtime EXPR†

Converts a time as returned by the **time** function to *ctime*(3) string. In array context, returns a 9-element array with the time analyzed for the local time zone.

oct EXPR†

Returns the decimal value of **EXPR** interpreted as an octal string. If **EXPR** starts off with 0x, interprets it as a hex string instead.

ord EXPR†

Returns the ascii value of the first character of **EXPR**.

vec EXPR, OFFSET, BITS

Treats string **EXPR** as a vector of unsigned integers, and yields the bit at **OFFSET**. **BITS** must be between 1 and 32. May be used as an *lvalue*.

Structure conversion

pack TEMPLATE, LIST

Packs the values into a binary structure using **TEMPLATE**.

unpack TEMPLATE, EXPR

Unpacks the structure **EXPR** into an array, using **TEMPLATE**.

TEMPLATE is a sequence of characters as follows:

a / A	Ascii string, null / space padded
b / B	Bit string in ascending / descending order
c / C	Native / unsigned char value
f / d	Single / double float in native format
h / H	Hex string, low / high nybble first.
i / I	Signed / unsigned integer value
l / L	Signed / unsigned long value
n / N	Short / long in network (big endian) byte order
s / S	Signed / unsigned short value
u / p	Uuencoded string / Pointer to a string
v / V	Short / long in VAX (little endian) byte order
x / @	Null byte / null fill until position
X	Backup a byte

Each character may be followed by a decimal number which will be used as a repeat count. '*' specifies all remaining arguments.

If the format is preceded with %N, **unpack** returns an N-bit checksum instead.

Spaces may be included in the template for readability purposes.

String functions

chomp LIST†

Removes line endings from all elements of the list; returns the (total) number of characters removed.

chop LIST†

Chops off the last character on all elements of the list; returns the last chopped character.

crypt PLAINTEXT, SALT

Encrypts a string.

eval EXPR†

EXPR is parsed and executed as if it were a Perl program. The value returned is the value of the last expression evaluated. If there is a syntax error or runtime error, an undefined string is returned by **eval**, and $@ is set to the error message. See also **eval** in section 'Miscellaneous'.

index STR, SUBSTR [, OFFSET]

Returns the position of **SUBSTR** in **STR** at or after **OFFSET**. If the substring is not found, returns -1 (but see $[in section 'Special variables').

length EXPR†

Returns the length in characters of the value of **EXPR**.

lc EXPR

>   Returns a lower case version of **EXPR**.

lcfirst EXPR

>   Returns **EXPR** with the first character in lower case.

quotemeta EXPR

>   Returns **EXPR** with all regexp meta-characters quoted.

rindex STR, SUBSTR [, OFFSET]

>   Returns the position of the last **SUBSTR** in **STR** at or before **OFFSET**.

substr EXPR, OFFSET [, LEN]

>   Extracts a substring out of **EXPR** and returns it. If **OFFSET** is negative, counts
>   from the end of the string. May be used as an it lvalue.

uc EXPR

>   Returns an upper case version of **EXPR**.

ucfirst EXPR

>   Returns **EXPR** with the first character in upper case.

Array and list functions

delete $HASH{KEY}

>   Deletes the specified value from the specified hash. Returns the deleted
>   value unless **HASH** is **tie**d to a package that does not support it.

each %HASH

>   Returns a 2-element array consisting of the key and value for the next value
>   of the hash. Entries are returned in an apparently random order. After all
>   values of the hash have been returned, a null array is returned. The next call
>   to **each** after that will start iterating again.

exists EXPR†

>   Checks if the specified hash key exists in its hash array.

grep EXPR, LIST
grep BLOCK LIST

>   Evaluates **EXPR** or **BLOCK** for each element of the **LIST**, locally setting $_ to
>   refer to the element. Modifying $_ will modify the corresponding element
>   from **LIST**. Returns the array of elements from **LIST** for which **EXPR** returned
>   **true**.

join EXPR, LIST

>   Joins the separate strings of **LIST** into a single string with fields separated by
>   the value of **EXPR**, and returns the string.

keys %HASH

>   Returns an array of all the keys of the named hash.

map EXPR, LIST
map BLOCK LIST

Evaluates **EXPR** or **BLOCK** for each element of the **LIST**, locally setting $_ to refer to the element. Modifying $_ will modify the corresponding element from **LIST**. Returns the list of results.

pop @ARRAY

Pops off and returns the last value of the array.

push @ARRAY, LIST

Pushes the values of **LIST** onto the end of **ARRAY**.

reverse LIST

In array context: returns the **LIST** in reverse order.
In scalar context: returns the first element of **LIST** with bytes reversed.

scalar @ARRAY

Returns the number of elements in the array.

scalar %HASH

Returns a **true** value if the hash has elements defined.

shift [@ARRAY]

Shifts the first value of the array off and returns it, shortening the array by 1 and moving everything down. If @ARRAY is omitted, shifts @ARGV in main and @_ in subroutines.

sort [SUBROUTINE] LIST

Sorts the **LIST** and returns the sorted array value. If **SUBROUTINE** is specified, gives the name of a subroutine that returns less than zero, zero, or greater than zero, depending on how the elements of the array, available to the routine as $a and $b, are to be ordered.
SUBROUTINE may be the name of a user-defined routine, or a **BLOCK**.

splice @ARRAY, OFFSET [, LENGTH [, LIST]]

Removes the elements of @ARRAY designated by **OFFSET** and **LENGTH**, and replaces them with **LIST** (if specified).
Returns the elements removed.

split [PATTERN [, EXPR† [, LIMIT]]]

Splits a string into an array of strings, and returns it. If **LIMIT** is specified, splits into at most that number of fields. If **PATTERN** is also omitted, splits on whitespace. If not in array context: returns number of fields and splits to @_.
See also: 'Search and replace functions'.

unshift @ARRAY, LIST

Prepends list to the front of the array, and returns the number of elements in the new array.

values %HASH

Returns a normal array consisting of all the values of the named hash.

Regular expressions

Each character matches itself, unless it is one of the special characters +?.*^$()[]{}|\. The special meanings of these characters can be escaped using a '\'.

.   matches an arbitrary character, but not a newline unless it is a single-line match (see **m//s**).

(...)   groups a series of pattern elements to a single element.

^   matches the beginning of the target. In multi-line mode (see **m//m**) also matches after every newline character.

$ matches the end of the line. In multi-line mode also matches before every newline character.

[...] denotes a class of characters to match. [^...] negates the class.

(...|...|...) matches one of the alternatives.

(?# **TEXT**) Comment.

(?: **REGEXP**) Like (**REGEXP**) but does not make back-references.

(?= **REGEXP**) Zero width positive look-ahead assertion.

(?! **REGEXP**) Zero width negative look-ahead assertion.

(? **MODIFIER**) Embedded pattern-match modifier. **MODIFIER** can be one or more of **i**, **m**, **s** or **x**.

Quantified subpatterns match as many times as possible. When followed with a '?' they match the minimum number of times. These are the quantifiers:

+   matches the preceding pattern element one or more times.

?   matches zero or one times.

*   matches zero or more times.

{N,M} denotes the minimum **N** and maximum **M** match count. {N} means exactly **N** times; {N,} means at least **N** times.

A '\' escapes any special meaning of the following character if *non*-alphanumeric, but it turns most alphanumeric characters into something special:

\w   matches alphanumeric, including '_', \W matches non-alphanumeric.

\s   matches whitespace, \S matches non-whitespace.

\d   matches numeric, \D matches non-numeric.

\A   matches the beginning of the string, \Z matches the end.

\b   matches word boundaries, \B matches non-boundaries.

\G   matches where the previous **m//g** search left off.

\n, \r, \f, \t etc. have their usual meaning.

\w, \s and \d may be used within character classes, \b denotes backspace in this context.

Back-references:

\1... \9 refer to matched sub-expressions, grouped with (), inside the match.

\10 and up can also be used if the pattern matches that many sub-expressions.

See also $1... $9, $+, $&, $' and $' in section 'Special variables'.

With modifier **x**, whitespace can be used in the patterns for readability purposes.

Search and replace functions

[EXPR =~] [m] /PATTERN/ [g] [i] [m] [o] [s] [x]

Searches **EXPR** (default: $_) for a pattern. If you prepend an **m** you can use almost any pair of delimiters instead of the slashes. If used in array context, an array is returned consisting of the sub-expressions matched by the parentheses in pattern, i.e. ($1,$2,$3,...).
Optional modifiers: **g** matches as many times as possible; **i** searches in a case-insensitive manner; **o** interpolates variables only once.
m treats the string as multiple lines; **s** treats the string as a single line; **x** allows for regular expression extensions.
If **PATTERN** is empty, the most recent pattern from a previous match or replacement is used.
With **g** the match can be used as an iterator in scalar context.

?PATTERN?

This is just like the /**PATTERN**/ search, except that it matches only once between calls to the **reset** operator.

[$VAR =~] s/PATTERN/REPLACEMENT/ [e] [g] [i] [m] [o] [s] [x]

Searches a string for a pattern, and if found, replaces that pattern with the replacement text. It returns the number of substitutions made, if any, otherwise it returns **false**.
Optional modifiers: **g** replaces all occurrences of the pattern; **e** evaluates the replacement string as a Perl expression; for the other modifiers, see /**PAT-TERN**/ matching. Almost any delimiter may replace the slashes; if single quotes are used, no interpolation is done on the strings between the delimiters, otherwise they are interpolated as if inside double quotes.
If bracketing delimiters are used, **PATTERN** and **REPLACEMENT** may have their own delimiters, e.g. s(foo)[bar].
If **PATTERN** is empty, the most recent pattern from a previous match or replacement is used.

[$VAR =~] tr/SEARCHLIST/REPLACEMENTLIST/ [c] [d] [s]

Translates all occurrences of the characters found in the search list with the corresponding character in the replacement list. It returns the number of characters replaced. **y** may be used instead of **tr**.

Optional modifiers: **c** complements the **SEARCHLIST**; **d** deletes all characters found in **SEARCHLIST** that do not have a corresponding character in RE-PLACEMENTLIST; **s** squeezes all sequences of characters that are translated into the same target character into one occurrence of this character.

pos SCALAR

Returns the position where the last **m//g** search left off for **SCALAR**. May be used as an lvalue.

study [$VAR†]

Studies the scalar variable **$VAR** in anticipation of performing many pattern matches on its contents before the variable is next modified.

File test operators

These unary operators take one argument, either a filename or a filehandle, and test the associated file to see if something is true about it. If the argument is omitted, they test $_ (except for -t, which tests STDIN). If the special argument _ (underscore) is passed, they use the info of the preceding test or **stat** call.

-r -w -x	File is readable/writable/executable by effective uid/gid.
-R -W -X	File is readable/writable/executable by real uid/gid.
-o -O	File is owned by effective/real uid.
-e -z	File exists/has zero size.
-s	File exists and has non-zero size. Returns the size.
-f -d	File is a plain file, a directory.
-l -S -p	File is a symbolic link, a socket, a named pipe (FIFO).
-b -c	File is a block/character special file.
-u -g -k	File has setuid/setgid/sticky bit set.
-t	Tests if filehandle (STDIN by default) is opened to a tty.
-T -B	File is a text/non-text (binary) file. -T and -B return **true** on a null file, or a file at EOF when testing a filehandle.
-M -A -C	File modification/access/inode change time. Measured in days. Value returned reflects the file age at the time the script started. See also $^T in section 'Special variables'.

File operations

Functions operating on a list of files return the number of files successfully operated upon.

chmod LIST

Changes the permissions of a list of files. The first element of the list must be the numerical mode.

chown LIST

Changes the owner and group of a list of files. The first two elements of the list must be the numerical uid and gid.

truncate FILE, SIZE

truncates FILE to SIZE. FILE may be a filename or a filehandle.

link OLDFILE, NEWFILE

Creates a new filename linked to the old filename.

lstat FILE

Like stat, but does not traverse a final symbolic link.

mkdir DIR, MODE

Creates a directory with given permissions. Sets $! on failure.

readlink EXPR†

Returns the value of a symbolic link.

rename OLDNAME, NEWNAME

Changes the name of a file.

rmdir FILENAME†

Deletes the directory if it is empty. Sets $! on failure.

stat FILE

Returns a 13-element array (0:$dev, 1:$ino, 2:$mode, 3:$nlink, 4:$uid, 5:$gid, 6:$rdev, 7:$size, 8:$atime, 9:$mtime, 10:$ctime, 11:$blksize, 12:$blocks). FILE can be a filehandle, an expression evaluating to a filename, or _ to refer to the last file test operation or **stat** call.
Returns a null list if the **stat** fails.

symlink OLDFILE, NEWFILE

Creates a new filename symbolically linked to the old filename.

unlink LIST

Deletes a list of files.

utime LIST

Changes the access and modification times. The first two elements of the list must be the numerical access and modification times.

Input / Output

In input/output operations, **FILEHANDLE** may be a filehandle as opened by the **open** operator, a pre-defined filehandle (e.g. STDOUT) or a scalar variable which evaluates to the name of a filehandle to be used.

<FILEHANDLE>

In scalar context: reads a single line from the file opened on **FILEHANDLE**. In array context: reads the whole file.

< >   Reads from the input stream formed by the files specified in @ARGV, or standard input if no arguments were supplied.

binmode FILEHANDLE

Arranges for the file opened on **FILEHANDLE** to be read or written in 'binary' mode as opposed to 'text' mode (null-operation on UNIX).

close FILEHANDLE

Closes the file or pipe associated with the file handle.

dbmclose %HASH

Deprecated, use **untie** instead.

dbmopen %HASH, DBMNAME, MODE

Deprecated, use **tie** instead.

eof FILEHANDLE

Returns 1 if the next read will return end of file, or if the file is not open.

eof   Returns the eof status for the last file read.

eof( )   Indicates eof on the pseudo-file formed of the files listed on the command line.

fcntl FILEHANDLE, FUNCTION, $VAR

Implements the *fcntl*(2) function. This function has non-standard return values. See the manual for details.

fileno FILEHANDLE

Returns the file descriptor for a given (open) file.

flock FILEHANDLE, OPERATION

Calls *flock*(2) on the file. **OPERATION** formed by adding 1 (shared), 2 (exclusive), 4 (non-blocking) or 8 (unlock).

getc [FILEHANDLE]

Yields the next character from the file, or " " on end of file.
If **FILEHANDLE** is omitted, reads from STDIN.

ioctl FILEHANDLE, FUNCTION, $VAR

performs *ioctl*(2) on the file. This function has non-standard return values. See the manual for details.

open FILEHANDLE [, FILENAME]

Opens a file and associates it with FILEHANDLE. If FILENAME is omitted, the scalar variable of the same name as the FILEHANDLE must contain the filename.

The following filename conventions apply when opening a file.

"FILE"	open FILE for input. Also **"<FILE"**.
">FILE"	open FILE for output, creating it if necessary.
">>FILE"	open FILE in append mode.
"+>FILE"	open FILE with read/write access.
" | CMD"	opens a pipe to command CMD. If CMD is '-', forks.
"CMD | "	opens a pipe from command CMD. If CMD is '-', forks.

FILE may be &FILEHND, in which case the new file handle is connected to the (previously opened) filehandle FILEHND. If it is &=N, FILE will be connected to the given file descriptor.

open returns **undef** upon failure, **true** otherwise.

pipe READHANDLE, WRITEHANDLE

Returns a pair of connected pipes.

print [FILEHANDLE] [LIST†]

Prints the elements of LIST, converting them to strings if needed. If FILEHAN-DLE is omitted, prints by default to standard output (or to the last selected output channel, see **select**).

printf [FILEHANDLE] LIST]

Equivalent to `print` FILEHANDLE `sprintf` LIST.

read FILEHANDLE, $VAR, LENGTH [, OFFSET]

Reads LENGTH binary bytes from the file into the variable at OFFSET. Returns number of bytes actually read.

seek FILEHANDLE, POSITION, WHENCE

Arbitrarily positions the file. Returns 1 upon success, 0 otherwise.

select [FILEHANDLE]

Returns the currently selected filehandle. Sets the current default filehandle for output operations if FILEHANDLE is supplied.

select RBITS, WBITS, NBITS, TIMEOUT

Performs a *select*(2) system call with the same parameters.

sprintf FORMAT, LIST

Returns a string formatted by (almost all of) the usual *printf*(3) conventions.

sysread FILEHANDLE, $VAR, LENGTH [, OFFSET]

Reads LENGTH bytes into $VAR at OFFSET.

syswrite FILEHANDLE, SCALAR, LENGTH [, OFFSET]

> Writes **LENGTH** bytes from **SCALAR** at **OFFSET**.

tell [FILEHANDLE]

> Returns the current file position for the file. If **FILEHANDLE** is omitted, assumes the file last read.

Formats

formline PICTURE, LIST

> Formats **LIST** according to **PICTURE** and accumulates the result into $ ˆ A.

write [FILEHANDLE]

> Writes a formatted record to the specified file, using the format associated with that file.

Formats are defined as follows:

format [NAME] =
FORMLIST
.

FORMLIST pictures the lines, and contains the arguments which will give values to the fields in the lines. **NAME** defaults to STDOUT if omitted.
Picture fields are:

> @<<<. . .   left adjusted field, repeat the < to denote the desired width;
> @>>>. . .   right adjusted field;
> @| | |. . .   centered field;
> @# . ##. . .   numeric format with implied decimal point;
> @*   a multi-line field.

Use ˆ instead of @ for multi-line block filling.

Use ˜ at the beginning of a line to suppress unwanted empty lines.

Use ˜˜ at the beginning of a line to have this format line repeated until all fields are exhausted.

Set $ - to zero to force a page break.

See also $ ˆ, $ ˜, $ ˆA, $ ˆF, $ - and $= in section 'Special variables'.

Directory reading routines

closedir DIRHANDLE

> Closes a directory opened by opendir.

opendir DIRHANDLE, DIRNAME

> Opens a directory on the handle specified.

readdir DIRHANDLE
> Returns the next entry (or an array of entries) in the directory.

rewinddir DIRHANDLE
> Positions the directory to the beginning.

seekdir DIRHANDLE, POS
> Sets position for readdir on the directory.

telldir DIRHANDLE
> Returns the postion in the directory.

System interaction

alarm EXPR
> Schedules a SIGALRM to be delivered after **EXPR** seconds.

chdir [EXPR]
> Changes the working directory.
> Uses $ENV{"HOME"} or $ENV{"LOGNAME"} if **EXPR** is omitted.

chroot FILENAME†
> Changes the root directory for the process and its children.

die [LIST]
> Prints the value of **LIST** to STDERR and exits with the current value of $!
> (errno). If $! is 0, exits with the value of ($? >> 8). If ($? >> 8) is 0,
> exits with 255. **LIST** defaults to "Died".

exec LIST
> Executes the system command in **LIST**; does not return.

exit [EXPR]
> Exits immediately with the value of EXPR, which defaults to 0 (zero). Calls
> END routines and object destructors before exiting.

fork Does a *fork*(2) system call. Returns the child pid to the parent process and
> zero to the child process.

getlogin
> Returns the current login name as known by the system.

getpgrp [PID]
> Returns the process group for process **PID** (0, or omitted, means the current
> process).

getppid
> Returns the process id of the parent process.

getpriority WHICH, WHO
> Returns the current priority for a process, process group, or user.

glob PAT

Returns a list of filenames that match the shell pattern **PAT**.

kill LIST

Sends a signal to a list of processes. The first element of the list must be the signal to send (numeric, or its name as a string).

setpgrp PID, PGRP

Sets the process group for the **PID** (0 = current process).

setpriority WHICH, WHO, PRIO

Sets the current priority for a process, process group, or a user.

sleep [EXPR]

Causes the script to sleep for **EXPR** seconds, or forever if no **EXPR**. Returns the number of seconds actually slept.

syscall LIST

Calls the system call specified in the first element of the list, passing the rest of the list as arguments to the call.

system LIST

Does exactly the same thing as **exec LIST** except that a fork is performed first, and the parent process waits for the child process to complete.

times

Returns a 4-element array (0:$user, 1:$system, 2:$cuser, 3:$csystem) giving the user and system times, in seconds, for this process and the children of this process.

umask [EXPR]

Sets the umask for the process and returns the old one. If **EXPR** is omitted, returns current umask value.

wait   Waits for a child process to terminate and returns the pid of the deceased process (-1 if none). The status is returned in **$?**.

waitpid PID, FLAGS

Performs the same function as the corresponding system call.

warn [LIST]

Prints the message on STDERR like **die**, but does not exit.
LIST defaults to "Warning: something's wrong".

Networking

accept NEWSOCKET, GENERICSOCKET

Accepts a new socket.

bind SOCKET, NAME

Binds the **NAME** to the **SOCKET**.

connect SOCKET, NAME
> Connects the **NAME** to the **SOCKET**.

getpeername SOCKET
> Returns the socket address of the other end of the **SOCKET**.

getsockname SOCKET
> Returns the name of the socket.

getsockopt SOCKET, LEVEL, OPTNAME
> Returns the socket options.

listen SOCKET, QUEUESIZE
> Starts listening on the specified **SOCKET**.

recv SOCKET, SCALAR, LENGTH, FLAGS
> Receives a message on **SOCKET**.

send SOCKET, MSG, FLAGS [, TO]
> Sends a message on the **SOCKET**.

setsockopt SOCKET, LEVEL, OPTNAME, OPTVAL
> Sets the requested socket option.

shutdown SOCKET, HOW
> Shuts down a **SOCKET**.

socket SOCKET, DOMAIN, TYPE, PROTOCOL
> Creates a **SOCKET** in **DOMAIN** with **TYPE** and **PROTOCOL**.

socketpair SOCKET1, SOCKET2, DOMAIN, TYPE, PROTOCOL
> As socket, but creates a pair of bi-directional sockets.

SystemV IPC

msgctl ID, CMD, ARGS
> Calls *msgctl*(2). If **CMD** is &IPC_STAT then **ARG** must be a variable.

msgget KEY, FLAGS
> Creates a message queue for **KEY**. Returns the message queue identifier.

msgsnd ID, MSG, FLAGS
> Sends **MSG** to queue **ID**.

msgrcv ID, $VAR, SIZE, TYPE, FLAGS
> Receives a message from queue **ID** into **VAR**.

semctl ID, SEMNUM, CMD, ARG
> Calls *semctl*(2).
> If **CMD** is &IPC_STAT of &GETALL then **ARG** must be a variable.

semget KEY, NSEMS, SIZE, FLAGS

Creates a set of semaphores for **KEY**. Returns the message semaphore identifier.

semop KEY, ...

Performs semaphore operations.

shmctl ID, CMD, ARG

Calls *shmctl*(2). If **CMD** is &IPC_STAT then **ARG** must be a variable.

shmget KEY, SIZE, FLAGS

Creates shared memory. Returns the shared memory segment identifier.

shmread ID, $VAR, POS, SIZE

Reads at most **SIZE** bytes of the contents of shared memory segment **ID** starting at offset **POS** into **VAR**.

shmwrite ID, STRING, POS, SIZE

Writes at most **SIZE** bytes of **STRING** into the contents of shared memory segment **ID** at offset **POS**.

Miscellaneous

defined EXPR

Tests whether the lvalue **EXPR** has an actual value.

do FILENAME

Executes **FILENAME** as a Perl script. See also **require** in section 'Subroutines, packages and modules'.

dump [LABEL]

Immediate core dump. When reincarnated, starts at **LABEL**.

eval {EXPR; . . . }

Executes the code between { and } . Traps run-time errors as described with **eval**(EXPR), section 'String functions' .

local LIST

Creates a scope for the listed variables local to the enclosing block, subroutine or eval.

my LIST

Creates a scope for the listed variables lexically local to the enclosing block, subroutine or eval.

ref EXPR†

Returns a **true** value if **EXPR** is a reference. Returns the package name if **EXPR** has been blessed into a package.

reset [EXPR]

Resets ?? searches so that they work again. **EXPR** is a list of single letters. All variables and arrays beginning with one of those letters are reset to their pristine state. Only affects the current package.

scalar EXPR

Forces evaluation of **EXPR** in scalar context.

undef [LVALUE]

Undefines the **LVALUE**. Always returns the undefined value.

wantarray

Returns **true** if the current context expects an array value.

Information from system files

See the manual about return values in scalar context.

passwd
Returns ($name, $passwd, $uid, $gid, $quota, $comment, $gcos, $dir, $shell).

endpwent	Ends look-up processing.
getpwent	Gets next information.
getpwnam NAME	Gets information by name.
getpwuid UID	Gets information by uid.
setpwent	Resets look-up processing.

group
Returns ($name, $passwd, $gid, $members).

endgrent	Ends look-up processing.
getgrgid GID	Gets information by group ID.
getgrnam NAME	Gets information by name.
getgrent	Gets next information.
setgrent	Resets look-up processing.

hosts
Returns ($name, $aliases, $addrtype, $length, @addrs).

endhostent	Ends look-up processing.
gethostbyaddr ADDR, ADDRTYPE	Gets information by address.
gethostbyname NAME	Gets information by name.

gethostent	Gets next information.
sethostent STAYOPEN	Resets look-up processing.

networks
Returns ($name, $aliases, $addrtype, $net).

endnetent	Ends look-up processing.
getnetbyaddr ADDR, TYPE	Gets information by address and type.
getnetbyname NAME	Gets information by name.
getnetent	Gets next information.
setnetent STAYOPEN	Resets look-up processing.

services
Returns ($name, $aliases, $port, $proto).

endservent	Ends look-up processing.
getservbyname NAME, PROTO	Gets information by name.
getservbyport PORT, PROTO	Gets information by port.
getservent	Gets next information.
setservent STAYOPEN	Resets look-up processing.

protocols
Returns ($name, $aliases, $proto).

endprotoent	Ends look-up processing.
getprotobyname NAME	Gets information by name.
getprotobynumber NUMBER	Gets information by number.
getprotoent	Gets next information.
setprotoent STAYOPEN	Resets look-up processing.

Special variables

The following variables are global and should be localized in subroutines:

$_   The default input and pattern-searching space.

$.   The current input line number of the last filehandle that was read.

$/   The input record separator, newline by default. May be multi-character.

$,   The output field separator for the print operator.

$ "   The separator which joins elements of arrays interpolated in strings.

$ \   The output record separator for the print operator.

$ #   The output format for printed numbers. Deprecated.

$ *   Set to 1 to do multiline matching within strings. Deprecated, see the **m** and **s** modifiers in section 'Search and replace functions'.

$?   The status returned by the last ' COMMAND ' , pipe close or **system** operator.

$]   The Perl version number.

$ [The index of the first element in an array, and of the first character in a substring. Default is 0. Deprecated.

$;   The subscript separator for multi-dimensional array emulation. Default is "\034".

$!   If used in a numeric context, yields the current value of errno. If used in a string context, yields the corresponding error string.

$ @   The Perl error message from the last **eval** or **do** EXPR command.

$:   The set of characters after which a string may be broken to fill continuation fields (starting with '^') in a format.

$ 0   The name of the file containing the Perl script being executed. May be assigned to.

$ $ The process number of the Perl running this script. Altered (in the child process) by **fork**.

$ <   The real uid of this process.

$ >   The effective uid of this process.

$ (The real gid of this process.

$)   The effective gid of this process.

$ ^A   The accumulator for **formline** and **write** operations.

$ ^D   The debug flags as passed to Perl using -D .

$ ^F   The highest system file descriptor, ordinarily 2.

$ ^I   In-place edit extension as passed to Perl using -i .

$ ^L   Formfeed character used in formats.

$ ^P   Internal debugging flag.

$ ^T   The time (as delivered by **time**) when the program started. This value is used by the file test operators -M, -A and -C.

$ ^W   The value if the -w option as passed to Perl.

$^X   The name by which this Perl was invoked.

The following variables are context dependent and need not be localized:

$%   The current page number of the currently selected output channel.

$=   The page length of the current output channel. Default is 60 lines.

$-   The number of lines remaining on the page.

$~   The name of the current report format.

$^   The name of the current top-of-page format.

$| If set to nonzero, forces a flush after every write or print on the output channel currently selected. Default is 0.

$ARGV The name of the current file when reading from < > .

The following variables are always local to the current block:

$&   The string matched by the last successful pattern match.

$'   The string preceding what was matched by the last successful match.

$'   The string following what was matched by the last successful match.

$+   The last bracket matched by the last search pattern.

$1...$9...   Contain the subpatterns from the corresponding sets of parentheses in the last pattern successfully matched. $10... and up are only available if the match contained that many subpatterns.

Special arrays

@ARGV   Contains the command line arguments for the script (not including the command name).

@EXPORT
       Names the methods a package exports by default.

@EXPORT_OK
       Names the methods a package can export upon explicit request.

@INC   Contains the list of places to look for Perl scripts to be evaluated by the **do FILENAME** and **require** commands.

@ISA   List of 'base classes' of a package.

@_   Parameter array for subroutines. Also used by **split** if not in array context.

%ENV   Contains the current environment.

%INC   List of files that have been included with **require** or **do**.

%OVERLOAD
       Can be used to overload operators in a package.

%SIG   Used to set signal handlers for various signals.

Environment variables

Perl uses the following environment variables.

HOME   Used if **chdir** has no argument.

LOGDIR
         Used if **chdir** has no argument and HOME is not set.

PATH   Used in executing subprocesses, and in finding the Perl script if -S is
         used.

PERL5LIB
         A colon-separated list of directories to look in for Perl library files before
         looking in the standard library and the current directory.

PERL5DB
         The command to get the debugger code.
         Defaults to BEGIN { require 'perl5db.pl' }.

PERLLIB
         Used instead of PERL5LIB if the latter is not defined.

The Perl debugger

The Perl symbolic debugger is invoked with 'perl -d'.

h   Prints out a help message.

T   Stack trace.

s   Single steps.

n   Single steps around subroutine call.

RET   Repeats last s or n.

r   Returns from the current subroutine.

c [LINE]   Continues (until LINE, or another breakpoint or exit).

p EXPR†   Prints EXPR.

l [RANGE] Lists a range of lines. RANGE may be a number, start-end,
             start+amount, or a subroutine name. If omitted, lists next window.

-            Lists previous window.

w   Lists window around current line.

f FILE   Switches to FILE and start listing it.

l SUB   Lists the named SUBroutine.

S   List the names of all subroutines.

/PATTERN/   Forward search for **PATTERN**.

?PATTERN?   Backward search for **PATTERN**.

b [LINE [CONDITION]]
                Sets breakpoint at **LINE**, default: current line.

b SUBNAME [CONDITION]
                Sets breakpoint at the subroutine.

d [LINE]   Deletes breakpoint at the given line.

D   Deletes all breakpoints.

L   Lists lines that have breakpoints or actions.

a LINE COMMAND
                Sets an action for line.

A   Deletes all line actions.

< COMMAND   Sets an action to be executed before every debugger prompt.

> COMMAND   Sets an action to be executed before every s, c or n command.

V [PACKAGE [VARS]]
                Lists all variables in a package. Default package is main.

X [VARS]   Like V, but assumes current package.

! [[-]NUMBER]
                Re-executes a debugging command. Default is previous command.

H [-NUMBER] Displays the last -**NUMBER** commands of more than one letter.

t   Toggles trace mode.

= [ALIAS VALUE]
                Sets alias, or lists current aliases.

q   Quits. You may also use your EOF character.

COMMAND   Executes **COMMAND** as a Perl statement.

HTML Quick Reference Guide

This section contains a reprint of the HTML Quick Reference Guide, as developed by Andrew Ford and Peter Fynn. It has been included in Andrew's book, *Spinning the Web* [Ford95] and Peter's book, *The WWW Handbook* [Flyn95].

It is reprinted here with permission of the authors.

HTML Quick Reference Guide

Spinning the Web   *The WorldWideWeb Handbook*
Andrew Ford   Peter Flynn
1–85032–141–8   1–85032–205–8

- Element names are not case sensitive
- Documents start with a `<!doctype>` statement, followed by a header and text body enclosed in `<html>...</html>`
- The header is enclosed in `<head>...</head>`
- The text body is enclosed in `<body>...</body>`
- Comments are written as `<!-- A comment -->`

Elements in dark gray are not in HTML 2.0 but are supported by browsers: elements in light gray are obsolescent. Optional attributes are given in [square brackets]. The full DTD can be found at http://www.w3.org/hypertext/WWW/MarkUp/MarkUp.html

Sample document

```
<!DOCTYPE HTML PUBLIC "-//IETF//DTD HTML//EN">
<html>
  <head> <!-- A sample document -->
    <title>Document title</title>
    <link rev="made" href="mailto:info@itpuk.co.uk">
  </head>
  <body>
    <h1>Top-level heading</h1>
    <p>First paragraph of text.</p>
    <ul> <!-- A bulleted list -->
      <li>First list item</li>
      <li>Second list item, with a hypertext
      <a href="info.html">link<a> to another file.</li>
    </ul> <h2>Second-level heading</h2>
    <p>Another paragraph, <img alt="Picture of me"
      align="bottom" src="mypic.gif">
      with an illustration.</p>
  </body>
</html>
```

Header elements

`<title>...</title>`	Document running title (not part of the text), recommended maximum length 64 characters
`<link ...>`	Relationships for the document as a whole: attributes `rel`, `rev`, `href`
`<base href="url">`	Defines the default structure for any partial (incomplete) URLs in the document
`<isindex>`	Document is a script which handles searches
`<meta ...>`	Embed meta-information for the server: attributes `http-equiv`, `name`, `content`
`<nextid n="#">`	Blank assigns next identifier to be generated

Section headings

<hn>...</hn> Section headings, six levels available <h1> to <h6>

Block-oriented elements

<p>...</p> Paragraphs of regular text
<address>...</address> Address information
<blockquote>...</blockquote> Block quotations (may contain paragraphs)
<pre>...</pre> Preformatted text (fixed-width characters)
<hr> Horizontal rule

Lists

<ol>...</ol> Ordered lists, items numbered consecutively
<ul>...</ul> Unordered lists, items bulleted
<menu>...</menu> Menu lists
<dir>...</dir> Directory lists
<li>...</li> List items within ordered, unordered, menu, and directory lists
<dl>...</dl> Definition lists
<dt>...</dt> Definition term in a definition list
<dd>...</dd> Definition discussion in a definition list, may contain other block-oriented elements

The <ol>, <ul>, <menu>, <dir>, and <dl> elements may have a compact attribute.

Inline elements

Logical markup

<cite>...</cite> *Citations*
<code>...</code> Computer code
<dfn>...</dfn> *Defining instance* (see HTML3)
<em>...</em> *Emphasis*
<kbd>...</kbd> **Keyboard input**
<samp>...</samp> Literal characters
<strike>...</strike> strike-out (see HTML3)
<strong>...</strong> **Strong emphasis**
<var>...</var> Variable name

Visual markup

<b>...</b> **Bold type**

 Forced linebreak
<i>...</i> *Italic type*
<tt>...</tt> Typewriter type
<u>...</u> Underlined

Hypertext links

<a href="*url*">...</a> Link to another document or resource
<a href="*url#label*">...</a> Link to a specific destination in another document
<a href="#*label*">...</a> Link to a specific destination in the same document
<a name="*label*">...</a> Labels the surrounded text as a target destination

An <a> element may contain both href and name attributes.

Uniform Resource Locators (URLs)

These specify the location of a resource for a hypertext link:

```
http://www.thomson.com:80/catalog/order.html?searchterm
```
one of...	↓	↓	↓	#location
http://	Internet server	directory	filename	options:
gopher://	hostname or IP	name		searching means
ftp://	address with			URL must be a
telnet://	optional port.			script; using a
mailto:	Email address.			location implies
news:	Newsgroup name.			target label

Note mailto: and news: have no double slash. exists (see <a>).

Images

External images are specified with the <a> element as hypertext links. Inline images are specified as **<img src="*url*"** [align="..."] [alt="..."] [ismap]>
The value of align can be top, middle or bottom. The alt attribute provides text for non-graphical users and is strongly recommended. An image map (clickable image) is an <img> with ismap inside an <a> element pointing to a server map file:

```
<a href="http://www.foo.bar/cgi-bin/imagemap/mypic">
  <img src="http://www.foo.bar/mypic.gif"
  alt="Image map" ismap> </a>
```

Forms

<form method="..." action="*url*">...</form>
The URL should be a script or may use mailto: The method is GET or POST, depending on how you want the data returned. Within a form, input fields are defined with:

- for multiline text input (surrounds prompting text):
  <textarea name="..." rows="*n*" cols="*n*">...</textarea>
- for single-line input: **<input name="..." type="..." [...]>**
  The type can be one of text, checkbox, radio, hidden, password, reset, or submit. Other attributes are align, checked, size, maxlength, src, and value. All <input> fields of a radio or checkbox group must have the same name.
- for menus: **<select name="..." [multiple]>...</select>**
  Options are given with **<option [value="..."]>...[</option>]** within the <select>...</select>. Individual options can have an attribute of selected or disabled. If no value is given, the element content is used.

Example form

```
<hr> <form method="GET"
action="http://www.foo.bar/cgi-bin/script">
  <p>Name: <input name="name" type="text" size="20"><br>
  Operating system: <select name="opsys"><option>Unix
  <option>VMS<option>Mac<option>DOS<option></select></p>
  <p><textarea name="comments" rows="4" columns="40">
      Please write your comments here...</textarea></p>
  <p><input type="submit"> <input type="reset"></p>
</form> <hr>
```

Special characters

`&lt;`	<	less-than symbol
`&gt;`	>	greater-than symbol
`&amp;`	&	ampersand
`&quot;`	"	unidirectional double quote
` `	⊔	non-breaking space
`&shy;`	-	soft hyphen

ISO Latin-1 characters

`&Agrave;`	À	capital A, grave accent	`&iuml;`	ï	small i, diæresis/umlaut
`&agrave;`	à	small a, grave accent	`&ETH;`	Ð	capital Eth, Icelandic
`&Aacute;`	Á	capital A, acute accent	`&eth;`	ð	small eth, Icelandic
`&aacute;`	á	small a, acute accent	`&Ntilde;`	Ñ	capital N, tilde
`&Acirc;`	Â	capital A, circumflex	`&ntilde;`	ñ	small n, tilde
`&acirc;`	â	small a, circumflex	`&Ograve;`	Ò	capital O, grave accent
`&Atilde;`	Ã	capital A, tilde	`&ograve;`	ò	small o, grave accent
`&atilde;`	ã	small a, tilde	`&Oacute;`	Ó	capital O, acute accent
`&Auml;`	Ä	capital A, diæresis/umlaut	`&oacute;`	ó	small o, acute accent
`&auml;`	ä	small a, diæresis/umlaut	`&Ocirc;`	Ô	capital O, circumflex
`&Aring;`	Å	capital A, ring	`&ocirc;`	ô	small o, circumflex
`&aring;`	å	small a, ring	`&Otilde;`	Õ	capital O, tilde
`&AElig;`	Æ	capital AE ligature	`&otilde;`	õ	small o, tilde
`&aelig;`	æ	small ae ligature	`&Ouml;`	Ö	capital O, diæresis/umlaut
`&Ccedil;`	Ç	capital C, cedilla	`&ouml;`	ö	small o, diæresis/umlaut
`&ccedil;`	ç	small c, cedilla	`&Oslash;`	Ø	capital O, slash
`&Egrave;`	È	capital E, grave accent	`&oslash;`	ø	small o, slash
`&egrave;`	è	small e, grave accent	`&Ugrave;`	Ù	capital U, grave accent
`&Eacute;`	É	capital E, acute accent	`&ugrave;`	ù	small u, grave accent
`&eacute;`	é	small e, acute accent	`&Uacute;`	Ú	capital U, acute accent
`&Ecirc;`	Ê	capital E, circumflex	`&uacute;`	ú	small u, acute accent
`&ecirc;`	ê	small e, circumflex	`&Ucirc;`	Û	capital U, circumflex
`&Euml;`	Ë	capital E, diæresis/umlaut	`&ucirc;`	û	small u, circumflex
`&euml;`	ë	small e, diæresis/umlaut	`&Uuml;`	Ü	capital U, diæresis/umlaut
`&Igrave;`	Ì	capital I, grave accent	`&uuml;`	ü	small u, diæresis/umlaut
`&igrave;`	ì	small i, grave accent	`&Yacute;`	Ý	capital Y, acute accent
`&Iacute;`	Í	capital I, acute accent	`&yacute;`	ý	small y, acute accent
`&iacute;`	í	small i, acute accent	`&THORN;`	Þ	capital Thorn, Icelandic
`&Icirc;`	Î	capital I, circumflex	`&thorn;`	þ	small thorn, Icelandic
`&icirc;`	î	small i, circumflex	`&szlig;`	ß	small sharp s, German sz
`&Iuml;`	Ï	capital I, diæresis/umlaut	`&yuml;`	ÿ	small y, diæresis/umlaut

HTML3

```
<!DOCTYPE HTML PUBLIC "-//IETF//DTD HTML 3.0//EN">
```

Header elements

`<style notation="...">...</style>` Encloses stylesheet information
`<range from="`*label*`" until="`*label*`">` Specifies range marked in text with
`<spot id="`*label*`">` elements

Structural markup

All structural elements can have `class`, `lang`, `id`, `clear` and `background` attributes. Heading and list-oriented elements can have `seqnum`, `dingbat`, `src`, and `nowrap`. The `align` attribute can be used to affect visual positioning (e.g. `align="center"`).

`<banner>...</banner>`	Encloses static information to remain on display
`<bq>...</bq>`	Synonymous with `<blockquote>`
`<div class="...">...</div>`	To mark divisions (chapter, section, etc)
`<lh>...</lh>`	In lists, supplies a list header or title before the first `<li>` or `<dt>`
`<note role="...">...</note>`	Identifies footnotes, sidenotes etc
`<spot id="label">`	Marks a reference point for `<range>`

Logical markup

`<a id="label">`	Use of `id` replaces name in anchors
`<abbrev>...</abbrev>`	Identifies an abbreviation
`<acronym>...</acronym>`	Identifies an acronym
`<au>...</au>`	Authors' names
`<del>...</del>`	Marks text as having been deleted but kept for reference purposes
`<dfn>...</dfn>`	*Defining instance*
`<ins>...</ins>`	Marks new text inserted
`<lang>...</lang>`	Identifies a language other than the basic one of the document
`<person>...</person>`	Personal names
`<q>...</q>`	Encloses quoted speech (adds "quotes" automatically)
`<sub align="...">...</sub>`	Subscripts
`<sup align="...">...</sup>`	Superscripts

Visual markup

`<big>...</big>`	Designates bigger text (see `<small>`)
`<s>...</s>`	Replaces `<strike>` for ~~strikeout text~~ (see also `<ins>` and `<del>`)
`<small>...</small>`	Designates smaller text (see `<big>`)
`<tabstop id="label">`	Sets tab stop at current location
`<tab to="label">`	Tabs to the labelled position

Figures

`<figure src="/url">...</figure>`	Encloses a figure
`<caption>...</caption>`	Supplies a caption
`<credit>...</credit>`	Supplies a credit

Within figures, `<a>` elements can have a shape attribute which identifies a polygon in the image that the user can click on:

```
<figure id="d69" src="http://abc.xyz.org/~pat/house.gif"
align="center">
  <caption align="bottom">My house</caption>
  <p>Picture of my mansion in the hills above
    Naples, note the <a href="fire.html"
    shape="rect 20,120,50,140">hole in the roof</a>
    where the lightning struck.</p>
  <credit>The local paper took this shot.</credit>
</figure>
```

Forms

`<input type="file"...>`	Allows uploading of files to a server, permitted types specified with accept

(change `enctype` of `<form>` to
`multipart/form-data`)

`<input type="scribble"...>` For pen input
`<input type="audio"...>` For sound input

Mathematics

`<math [model="..."]>...</math>` Encloses a formula
`<box>...</box>` Surrounds symbols to be treated as a whole, optional `delim` attribute
`<over>` and `<atop>` Separate lined and unlined fractions
`<above>...</above>` Identifies numerator
`<below>...</below>` Identifies denominator
`<root root="`*n*`">` Root, degree specified as *n*
`<array>...</array>` LATEX-like arrays
`<arow>...</arow>` Row within an array
`<item>...</item>` Item within a row in an array

To minimize typing, `<sub>` and `<sup>` tags can be replaced with the underscore (_) and caret (^) respectively, and `<box>` tags can be replaced with {curly braces}, e.g. E=mc^2^

Tables

`<table [border]>...</table>` Defines a table
`<caption>...</caption>` Supplies a caption
`<tr>...</tr>` Encloses a table row
`<th>...</th>` Encloses a column or row header inside a row
`<td>...</td>` Encloses table data (a cell value)

```
<table border>
  <tr><th>Item</thi><th>Quantity</th></tr>
  <tr><th>Population</th></td>384,000</td></tr>
  <tr><th>Sample</th></td>384</td></tr>
  <caption>Fig 1. Survey Frame</caption> </table>
```

The `<th>` and `<td>` elements can have `align` and `span` attributes.

Additional characters from ISO 8859-1

Code	Entity	Glyph	Description	Code	Entity	Glyph	Description
			non-breaking space	&#177;	&plusmn;	±	plus-or-minus sign
&#161;	&iexcl;	¡	inv. exclamation mark	&#178;	&sup2;	2	superscript two
&#162;	&cent;	¢	cent sign	&#179;	&sup3;	3	superscript three
&#163;	&pound;	£	pound sign	&#180;	&acute;	´	acute accent
&#164;	&curren;	¤	general currency sign	&#181;	&micro;	µ	micro sign
&#165;	&yen;	¥	yen sign	&#182;	&para;	¶	pilcrow (paragraph)
&#166;	&brvbar;	¦	broken (vertical) bar	&#183;	&middot;	·	middle dot
&#167;	&sect;	§	section sign	&#184;	&cedil;		cedilla
&#168;	&uml;	¨	umlaut/dieresis	&#185;	&sup1;	1	superscript one
&#169;	&copy;	©	copyright sign	&#186;	&ordm;	º	ordinal indicator, male
&#170;	&ordf;	ª	ordinal indicator, fem	&#187;	&raquo;	»	angle quotation, right
&#171;	&laquo;	«	angle quotation, left	&#188;	&frac14;	$1/4$	fraction one-quarter
&#172;	&not;	¬	not sign	&#189;	&frac12;	$1/2$	fraction one-half
&#173;	&shy;	-	soft hyphen	&#190;	&frac34;	$3/4$	fraction three-quarters
&#174;	&reg;	®	registered sign	&#191;	&iquest;	¿	inv. question mark
&#175;	&macr;	¯	macron	&#215;	&times;	×	Multiply sign
&#176;	&deg;	°	degree sign	&#247;	&divide;	÷	Division sign

Copies of this card can be downloaded in PostScript and `.dvi` format for A4 and Letter size stationery from `ftp://ftp.thomson.com/itcp/WebExtras/` using anonymous FTP. Information about ITCP's titles can be obtained from `http://www.thomson.com/intlitcp.html`.

Bibliography

[Albi92]   Albitz, P. and Liu, C. (1992) *DNS and BIND*, O'Reilly & Associates, Inc,
             California.

[Codd70]   Codd, E.F. (1970) *A Relational Model of Data for Large Shared Data
             Banks*, CACM, **13**(6).

[Come88]   Comer, D. (1988) *Internetworking with TCP/IP*, Prentice-Hall, New
             Jersey.

[Cost93]   Costales, B., Allman, E. and Rickert, N (1993) *Sendmail*, O'Reilly &
             Associates, Inc, California.

[Cron94]   Cronin, M.J. (1994) *Doing Business on the Internet*, Van Nostrand
             Reinhold, New York.

[Dece94]   December, J. and Randall, N. (1994) *The World Wide Web Unleashed*,
             SAMS Publishing, Indiana.

[Dijk65]   Dijkstra, E.W. (1965) Co-operating sequential processes. *Program-
             ming Languages*, Academic Press, London.

[Flyn95]   Flynn, P. (1995) *The World Wide Web Handbook*, International Thom-
             son Computer Press, London.

[Ford95]   Ford, A. (1995) *Spinning the Web*, International Thomson Publishing,
             London.

[Hunt92]   Hunt, C. (1992) *TCP/IP Network Administration*, O'Reilly & Associates,
             Inc, California.

[Liu94]   Liu, C., Peek, J., Jones, R., Buus, B. and Nye, A. (1994) *Managing
             Internet Information Services*, O'Reilly & Associates, Inc, California.

[Neme95]   Nemeth, E., Snyder, G. and Seebass, S. (1995) *UNIX System Adminis-
             tration Handbook*, 2nd edn, Prentice-Hall, New Jersey.

[Schw92]   Schwartz, R. (1992) *Learning Perl*, O'Reilly & Associates, Inc, Califor-
             nia.

[Stei95]   Stein, L.D. (1995) *How to Set Up and Maintain a World Wide Web Site*,
             Addison Wesley, Reading MA.

[Stev90]   Stevens, W.R. (1990) *UNIX Network Programming*, Prentice-Hall, New Jersey.

[Tane87]   Tanenbaum, A.S. (1997) *Operating Systems: Design and Implementation*, Prentice-Hall, New Jersey.

[Wall90]   Wall, L. and Schwartz, R. (1990) *Programming Perl*, O'Reilly & Associates, Inc, California.

Index

access chart, 74
access statistics, 73, 76
acronyms, indexing of, 71
Archie, 22
authentication, 8, 18, 34, 86, 91, 100

Bourne shell, 31

C, 5
C Shell, 31
caching, 20
    of dynamic documents, 22
cataloging documents, 64
CERN, 1, 2, 11, 71, 116
CERN server, 53, 150
CGI, 4, 10, 12, 21, 31, 37, 86
    data parsing, 39
    environment variables, 33, 52, 55
        AUTH_TYPE, 34
        CONTENT_LENGTH, 34, 35
        CONTENT_TYPE, 34
        GATEWAY_INTERFACE, 33
        PATH_INFO, 33, 34, 91, 116
        PATH_TRANSLATED, 33, 34
        QUERY_STRING, 34, 35, 39, 40, 46
        REMOTE_ADDR, 34
        REMOTE_HOST, 34
        REMOTE_IDENT, 34
        REMOTE_USER, 34
        REQUEST_METHOD, 33, 41
        SCRIPT_NAME, 34, 51, 60, 79, 82
        SERVER_NAME, 33
        SERVER_PORT, 33
        SERVER_PROTOCOL, 33
        SERVER_SOFTWARE, 33

name–value pairs, 26, 39, 40, 46, 51, 111
programs, *see* gateway programs
scripts, *see* gateway programs
standard routines, 39, 143
    cgiparse, 40, 46, 47, 51, 58, 81
    html_end, 41, 81
    html_start, 41, 81
    lockfile, 42, 60
    send_header, 41
    sendmail, 44, 59
    timetolog, 43, 73
    timetostr, 43
    url_decode, 39
    url_encode, 39
cgi-lib.pl, 144
CGI.pm, 138, 144
coffee machine, 9
Common Gateway Interface, *see* CGI
concurrency control, 95, 113
    concurrent file access, 42, 86
    critical regions, 42, 98
    file locking, 42, 110, 113, 116, 141, 170
    over NFS, 43
    mutual exclusion, 98
    semaphores, 98
critical region, *see* concurrency control

database systems, 86, 103, 127
date conversion, 43
DBM files, 95, 103, 160, 170
DBperl, *see* Perl, common database interface
DELETE method, *see* HTTP
DNS, 13

193